CANADA'S
MYSTERY MAN
OF HIGH FINANCE

Dorothy Johnston Killam

Izaak Walton Killam

CANADA'S
MYSTERY MAN
OF HIGH FINANCE

The story of Izaak Walton Killam
and his glittering wife Dorothy

DOUGLAS HOW

LANCELOT PRESS
HANTSPORT, NOVA SCOTIA

ISBN 0-88999-305-X
Published 1986

Lancelot Press Limited, Hantsport, Nova Scotia
Office and plant situated on Highway No. 1, ½ mile east of Hantsport

PREFACE

Dorothy Killam would have loved it. Her husband would have been uncomfortable, just being there. To Zena Cherry, it was worth an entire column in the *Globe and Mail*, which began as follows:

> The Izaak Walton Killam Memorial Prizes for 1986 were presented by Maureen Forrester, chairman of the Canada Council, to professors Jacques Genest, W. Howard Rapson and Karel Wiesner at a gala dinner at Toronto's L'Hotel. The most illustrious of the council's Killam awards, the prizes honor eminent Canadian scholars actively engaged in research, be it in industry, government agencies or universities.

Each year the awards are made in a different city, and this was Toronto's turn, and a gala occasion it was. The presidents of the University of Toronto and York University gave a reception. The guest list sparkled with academic and other distinctions. The three winners were distinction itself: the University of Montreal's Dr. Genest one of the leaders in the development of modern clinical medicine; the University of Toronto's Dr. Rapson a leader for more than 40 years in international pulp and paper research; the University of New Brunswick's Dr. Wiesner internationally acclaimed for pioneering research in physical and organic chemistry.

Dorothy Killam would have loved it all because she loved these social affairs and, more importantly, this was the sort of occasion that said quite clearly that what her husband and she had wanted to do with the Killam millions was being done. It was happening. Each of the three awards alone was worth $50,000, and they were only the brightest and the best of those the Canada Council gave in the Killams' name. Annually, too, four universities and the Montreal Neurological Institute gave others. In all, Killam awards had benefitted some 4,000 scholars in numerous academic fields, their total value had risen close to $50,000,000, and the capital funds were there to see that they went on indefinitely.

It is doubtful that many of those in attendance at L'Hotel spent much time thinking about the Killams, he dead since 1955, and she since 1965, neither of whom had ever gone to university. The strange thing, if you knew their story, was that in their lifetimes it would have seemed unlikely that this sort of occasion could ever happen at all.

Yet it did, and it will be repeated many times.

This is their story. It has not been an easy one to put together because they left not a file, not a letter, not a single memo behind. They took most of their secrets to the grave after fascinating lives that had provided jobs to thousands, but in the end what was most important was this: it is doubtful that any couple in Canadian history has done more to help enrich the nation's intellectual life.

CONTENTS

1

A   PATRICIAN   BALANCE

It was, without doubt, a grand occasion. No less than three trains had come down the coast from Halifax to Liverpool, "three all-Pullman trains, equipped with dining cars," all specials, all crowded with invited dignitaries, from Premier E.N. Rhodes on down. At a luncheon, the web of speeches spun on and on, seven of them, and many messages were read. There was pride and hope and approbation in them all. This 14th day of December, 1929, it was agreed unanimously, was a momentous one for industry-hungry Nova Scotia — the day she formally welcomed into existence an industry that would rank second only to the steel-coal complex in Cape Breton.

It was true that the stock market had broken in New York in very recent weeks; it was true that the pulp and paper business had grown too fast and was passing through difficult times; but neither fact was allowed to cast too much of a pall over the ceremonies. The new mill of Mersey Paper Company Limited had seaboard and other advantages of its own. It could compete, and now that it was ready it was time for celebration.

Around the gathered hundreds of people stood the basis of it all, the plant that would pump fresh life into the frail economy of the province's South Shore, provide a market for the pulpwood farmers cut off their rocky lands when the crops

9

were in and the snow had come, provide for hundreds of Nova Scotians manufacturing jobs that had gone too long to others. The project had cost — mill and power supply combined — $18,000,000. The mill had been built in little more than 17 months, in record time and on schedule, and it had been built with a degree of excellence that would lead an expert to call it the best two-machine plant in Canada. Now its gaunt smokestack towered over the piles of wood, the machines designed to produce 250 tons of newsprint a day, the red brick buildings, the general offices, the stores department, the locomotive house, the roll grinder room and sub-stations, the slasher mill, the chipper room and other elements of the mill itself, over the new wharf, over the new C.N.R. siding. In every sense it was an operating entity.

Behind the plant, ranging miles inland from the sea, stood the evergreen forests that guaranteed it a supply of wood. Behind it, too, coursing down from the gentle hills, ran the Mersey, not the greatest river in the world by any means but the greatest in Nova Scotia, and tapped now by the provincial government for that vital ingredient: power. The planners had done their work. A leading architect had done his work. The engineers and builders had done theirs. The first company-owned ship had arrived from England to start its career carrying Mersey's newsprint to markets in great cities down the coast in the United States. It was true that Nova Scotia had not shared much in the flamboyant boom of the '20s, true that this South Shore area in particular had stumbled through two whole generations of economic stagnation, but now a new decade and a new day were about to dawn simultaneously.

At the luncheon, one speech after another struck that note. "This great industry," said the Premier, "will have a marked bearing upon the prosperity and development of the province . . . We have entered upon a new era of prosperity, the effects of which are seen on every hand and to this, our second largest industry, we may look with confidence for a stimulation of its growth and development for all time." Said another speaker: "It can be said with confidence that nothing has contributed so much to lift the gloom and brighten the horizon in Nova Scotia."

The opening ceremony itself, said a newspaper account, took place in the spacious machine shop, "with all its mechanical equipment stilled . . . Near the doors leading through the main mill buildings stood a specially constructed stand, effectively draped with the Union Jack and Nova Scotia's own flag, to which was affixed the golden button which was to set the wheels in motion. . . It was a dramatic moment when the Premier stepped up to the stand and pressed the button. Among the visitors and within the mill, complete silence reigned. Then suddenly, as if by magic, came the hum of machinery. In the machine shop itself, all the equipment was set in motion and then, coming as a most effective climax, the great doors leading to the main mill were thrown open and the hum of the great pulp and paper-making machines swept through the buildings." The initial silence gave way to cheering and applause. Suddenly everybody was shouting.

And everybody, it seemed, was there who had cause to be there, everybody that is but the most crucial figure of all, the man who had made the final, lonely decision that Mersey was a valid economic proposition, who had raised the millions of dollars to give it birth, who had staked his reputation on its future only relatively few years after another, kindred project, far away in the valleys of Quebec, had come crashing down around him and seemed to have destroyed him as a young mastermind of high finance. Mersey was, above all, Izaak Walton Killam's project, a less ambitious one than the other perhaps but still a crowning symbol of his restoration to eminence, his comeback — and his faith in his native province.

One speaker after another lauded him. "All praise is due to him," said the Premier, "for his courage, tenacity and vision in furnishing the large amount of capital required and in arranging for successful management and organization." Said Colonel Hugh Jones, Mersey's first manager: "The building of this mill was unique in many ways. Its financing under Mr. Killam's direction is correspondingly unique in that he built the mill and saw it in operation before he asked the public to invest in it. His has been the venture and his the courage to put it through."

Izaak Walton Killam was supposed to have been in Liverpool, or more accurately in tiny nearby Brooklyn, to hear

11

these words. His name had been on the list of distinguished guests, but he had sent word that he would be unable to attend. Instead he had sent a message expressing his appreciation to all those who had made the occasion possible, "not only for what you have done but for the very enthusiastic and cheerful spirit that has prevailed throughout." He was, he said, "indeed disappointed" that an injury to his eye had made it impossible for him to attend.

For those who knew him, it was no great surprise that he was not there. The truth, they suspected, probably had little or nothing to do with his eye. The fact was that he would have been expected to make a speech, and he never liked making speeches, never liked the limelight, even hated to have his picture taken. He was a shy man, a reserved man, a man of mystery. Indeed for years he would be known as "the mystery man of Canadian finance," an enigmatic figure, a man with a reputation for being secretive, cold, tough, brilliant but primarily unknown, a man who built a substantial empire peculiarly his own that ranged from Newfoundland to British Columbia and into various parts of Latin America and the Caribbean, who built it mainly on the twin pillars of power and pulp and paper but encompassing, too, public utilities, chocolates, sugar, films, real estate, a newspaper, grain and other things.

He was an ex-newsboy who came from a modest home, who with a high school education and sheer hard work taught himself to talk on even terms, in their own language, with accountants, bankers, engineers and lawyers. He was a man who knew his reputation, and let it be. He was a builder, a man who thought for the long haul, who thought in millions the way most men think in dollars. He was, beyond question, one of the giants of Canadian financial history and when he died, at 70 in 1955, he was called the richest man in Canada. Then came the strangest twist of all. This glacial man who had become noted for his dislike of taxes, who was never known in his lifetime as a generous giver, poured tens of millions of dollars into the enrichment of Canadian life. It was done through government use of the massive death taxes he refused to avoid and, 10 years later, through bequests in the will of an extraordinary wife who followed the broad outlines of his own thought.

12

Years after he'd gone people still wondered about him. It was doubtful that more than a very few ever really knew him, even among men who worked most closely with him, who knew of his numerous quiet kindnesses, who had a deep respect for his integrity, an admiring awe of his skills. Probably very few people ever really knew why he did the things he did, because he very seldom said. He played his cards close to the vest with an inscrutable poker face men found impossible to read. He was, in his sister's words, "a very private person."

"I am known in Montreal financial circles," he once said, "as a man who plays a lone hand." He was, in truth, a loner, and he went a loner's way.

Not so his wife Dorothy. By the time Mersey opened Killam had been married to her for seven years, and she *was* an extraordinary woman, 15 years younger than he, attractive, intelligent, elegant, as outgoing as he was withdrawn. Together, they formed a patrician balance between introvert and extrovert. She had flair, panache, could be imperious, could be gracious and friendly and kind. She doted on baseball, jewelry, the high life that would take her in splendor from one home to another, five in all, with servants in each. She would become famous as the woman who tried to buy major league baseball's Brooklyn Dodgers before their reincarnation in Los Angeles. To a friend, she "lived a fairytale life with herself as the princess."

Killam came from a prominent family but a relatively modest home in Yarmouth, N.S. She came from a Missouri family with an unusual orientation towards both God and Mammon. Her father, John Thomas Morris Johnston, was simultaneously both a banker and a preacher. The son of a Baptist minister, he was left an orphan at 12, went to Indian territory in what is now eastern Oklahoma, herded cattle and at 14 became a school teacher. At 16 he went home to Boone County, clerked in a store, then bought it at 19. At 27, he started a bank in his home town, Ashland, and was its president for years, even after he went into the ministry.

His parents wanted him to become a minister, so he took several years out for theological studies, was ordained at 31 and from 1887-1897 was a pastor in Jefferson City, the state capital. All that time he was chaplain of the Missouri Senate

13

and for two years chaplain at the state penitentiary. In fact, his daughter once said it was a visit to a prison that first convinced him he wanted to be a preacher.

From 1897 to 1907 he was pastor of a St. Louis church, and it was during this time, in 1899, that Dorothy was born. The family moved from there to Liberty, Mo., when the father became a professor of biography and history at William Jewell College. In 1910 he organized and for some years presided over a bank, the National Reserve, in Kansas City. By that time he no longer held a pastorate but did preach frequently.

He not only continued to preside over the Ashland bank but established others in Denison, Texas, and Muskogee, Oklahoma, and eventually returned to St. Louis to be associated with a trust company headed by his only son. He wrote four books, made *Who's Who in America*, and won a warm eulogy from one of the most prominent politicians in America.

Champ Clark, noted Speaker of the House of Representatives, once said, "There are two men to whom I never talk; I simply ask them questions." One was the Rev. Dr. Johnston, himself a Democrat who advised Clark and others on such matters as currency questions when they were considering a Federal Reserve Act. Said Clark: "Dr. Johnston, a preacher, had enough sense to make $3,000,000 to $4,000,000." That was in 1914, and the St. Louis *Post-Dispatch* said that after that he "engaged in many financial operations." But at the time the good Dr. Johnston said Clark's estimate was high; he personally doubted that his worth would amount to more than a million.

Thus daughter Dorothy would have known him as a well-to-do minister-teacher-banker. His wife was the former Florence Brooks, and the daughter liked to call herself Dorothy Brooks Johnston. The upbringing they gave her left its mark. She could quote at length from the Bible, and she always kept one at her bedside, a treasured one her father had given her. But it was perhaps the combination of being both the daughter and the wife of financial men that prepared her in a singular way for the climactic phase of her life. It saw her take over Killam's fortune and more than double it in a decade, greatly to the advantage of Canada.

2

THE YARMOUTH

CONNECTION

The Killam family traced its lineage back to Yorkshire, England. It was said that its members had lived there since the time of William the Conqueror, and that the name was once spelled as the Norman French Chillon, later as Killom. It was spelled Kilham — there is a parish of that name in Yorkshire's West Riding — when Augustine or Austin Kilham, his wife Alice and their children emigrated to the infant colony of Massachusetts in 1637. It was Killam by the time their descendant John Killam, his wife and two sons left Wenham, Mass., in 1766 to migrate to the Yarmouth area of Nova Scotia as part of New England's response to government urging to take up land now that French-speaking Acadians had been expelled. They settled at the head of tidewater on the Chegoggin River where they had been given a grant. Added to other lands acquired in the township it gave them a total of 983 acres.

In the way the family kept track of its evolution, John Killam had been known in Massachusetts as John the sixth. In his new surroundings, he promptly became John the first, and one of his seven sons John the second. There were eleven children in all, and from the sons stemmed a prolific Killam progeny.

John the second, Izaak Walton Killam's great grandfather, married Sarah Allen in 1794. They had eight children, and this branch of the family in particular developed a hardnosed way with the dollar in a Yarmouth that was, for years, a good place to make a dollar. It lay on the sea, at the south-western tip of that elongated wharf that is Nova Scotia, and through much of the 19th century it took bountiful advantage of its strategic location on the sea lanes of the world. Indeed, in the days of wooden ships and iron men, the days of Bluenose skippers whose harsh discipline and crack seamanship were bywords in the ports of the world, no place took greater advantage. By 1876, a local history records, Nova Scotia stood at the head of the shipping lists among the provinces of Canada, with 2,787 vessels registered, and Yarmouth was "unrivalled among the Ports of the world in the value and tonnage of her Shipping, proportionate to her population."

The development went well back into the 18th century, and in only one year after 1825 had the tonnage of the port suffered a decrease. By 1876, wrote local historian J. Murray Lawson, there were 280 vessels owned in Yarmouth. And the figures were still growing. "It is not too much to say," Lawson stressed, "that the genius of the place is a maritime genius. In the private offices, and insurance parlours, and to a large extent in the halls and reception rooms of private dwellings may be seen the omnipresent marine picture, representing some 'gay and gallant bark' whose voyages have yielded wealth and prosperity to its owner."

The real cause of all this, he wrote, "may be traced to the fact that, in the long run, shipping has been found to pay excellent dividends on the capital invested. The community has come to understand the requirements of commerce, and has adapted itself to them."

From Yarmouth's shipping sprang a number of fortunes, a number of business offshoots, large, handsome wooden homes with cupolas or widows' walks where women could watch their men coming and going beneath the white sails of full-rigged ships, barques, brigs, barquentines, sloops and schooners. Shipping developed a stately and prosperous little town of 8,000 noted for its trim hedges, gardens and trees, its white fences; in 1911 when Yarmouth was 150 years old a souvenir booklet would look back nostalgically upon these

16

days when it was "one of the richest small towns in the world." Shipping also produced "many instances of suffering and bravery, of shipwreck, death and rescue as well as hair's breadth escapes from dangers that seemed insurmountable." By 1876 close to 600 Yarmouth vessels had been lost at sea, "while harrowing tales of shipwreck had become familiar."

As part of all this, John Killam had built a 160-ton brig, *Trinidad*, in 1829. His brother Samuel had built a 247-ton brig, *Andrea*, in 1837. In 1841, at the age of 39, John's son Thomas — Izaak Walton Killam's grandfather — had built the 41-ton schooner *Margaret*, a year later the 244-ton brig *Elizabeth* and he'd gone on from there. In 1849, in league with his son George and W.K. Dudman, he formed Thomas Killam & Co.; then in 1862 the partnership was dissolved and he again went on his own. He became, said a Yarmouth newspaper, "one of the most successful shipowners and businessmen of the town." Over a period of half a century he and his heirs built or owned some 60 vessels and sent them out in trade to many parts of the world. To a number of them Thomas Killam gave South American names, *Brazil, Uruguay, Peru, Lima, Ecuador* and others, and they reflected the scope of his enterprise — and, prophetically, the scope of the enterprise of his grandson.

There is still a picture of old Thomas in the Killam Brothers office in Yarmouth — the picture of a thin-faced, white-haired, white-bearded patriarch. Politically he was a Liberal, and an active one; he even named one of his ships *Liberal.* For many years he sat in the Provincial House of Assembly, and when Nova Scotia fell into bitter debate over Confederation he was in the forefront. He was against Confederation, especially without that vote by the people which was never granted, suspicious of it as a Liberal, suspicious of it as a man accustomed to looking outward to the sea and ships rather than inland towards a proposed new country gradually being webbed together by railways.

At a "large and intelligent" joint public meeting at the Yarmouth courthouse on July 1, 1867, the day the new country was born, he deprecated the manner in which Confederation had been carried and he saw little cause for rejoicing among Nova Scotians. The province had "not been treated fairly," he said, and although he had intended to retire from public life such was "the present crisis" that he had decided to yield to solicitations that he run in the first federal election. Around him were the bizarre reflections of approbation for his views: flags at half-mast, men with black weeds in their hats, effigies of Conservative Charles Tupper, *the* Nova Scotian Father of Confederation, one of them beside a live rat. At night there was a burlesque parade that struck the same vivid note.

Thomas Killam's supporters went to the polls in September and they gave him nearly a 2-1 majority. Liberals won everywhere in Nova Scotia except in Cumberland County where Tupper survived the storm. But the thing that made Killam different from almost all the other elected men was that he refused to take his seat in the new Parliament in Ottawa. On the night of the 21st, when he was formally declared elected, he addressed a jubilant audience. The Nova Scotia returns, he said, had "proved the hostility of the people to Confederation and the manner in which it was forced on them." It would be a lesson "to legislators in future not to disregard the sentiments and wishes of the people."

Thomas Killam died in December 1868, at the age of 66, died without taking his seat in Ottawa and, so the story goes, convinced that Confederation could only mean slavery for Nova Scotians. In tribute, the weekly *Herald*, Liberal to the core, ran its two inside pages with black borders down every column, and the editor wrote that in doing so he felt he was "giving outward expression to the feelings of thousands of our readers." Thomas Killam had been "an honest, faithful man who loved his county and desired its prosperity" but such was the editor's own sense of regret that, for the moment at least, he simply could not pen a suitable eulogy to the deceased as "a politician, a man of commercial enterprise and promoter of the industrial interests of the county." In Halifax, less in disarray, the *Chronicle* paid tribute to Thomas Killam's "virtues, sensible and practical," and his "great earnestness"; it might truly be said that few men had ever more completely commanded the attention of the provincial Assembly. The *Halifax Citizen* commended him for his "firm and independent stand" on Confederation, and said that in business life Thomas Killam had been "noted for superior enterprise and liberality.

Having accumulated wealth by directing his attention to commercial pursuits, he evinced the generosity which gives to riches their highest dignity and best reward. There are men in Yarmouth today on the high road to fortune who owe their first step in life to Mr. Killam's liberality."

He died leaving an estate valued at $150,000 which by the time his widow died in 1895 had grown to $359,000, a very considerable sum in those days. The documents with his will tend to underline the *Citizen's* words. Certainly a good number of people owed him money.

Despite 21 years in politics, Thomas Killam had never been much for making speeches. But his son Frank was and he ran in the 1869 by-election for the seat his father had never taken. He said he too was dissatisfied "with the means used in obtaining the passage of the (British) North America Act and with many of its provisions." He would fight for severance of Nova Scotia from Confederation but "while this Province remains in the Union" he would favor "all projects for reform and progress without regarding what political party may originate them." He won the seat, and from then to 1882 he sat in it, acquiring a considerable reputation as a "silver-tongued orator."

He was one of nine members of the Thomas Killam family, six of them sons, and he and two of his brothers, John and Thomas, carried on the family business. They reorganized it in 1869 as Killam Brothers, describing themselves as "successors to the late Thomas Killam" and as doing business as "Importers and Wholesale Dealers in West India Produce and General Commission Agents." The firm is still there, in the same gray wooden building down by the waterfront. It's always been run by Killams and when it was 100 years old, in 1949, a Yarmouth paper paid tribute to it as the oldest business in town. It had started, under Thomas, mainly in the line of ship chandlers or suppliers, and that had gone. The Brothers were organized "mainly as West Indian merchants," and that line of business had gone too. By 1949 it was involved in fuel supplies and insurance. Well into the 1980's it still was.

The last child of Thomas Killam, William Dudman, was born in 1857, so he was only 11 years old when his father died and 12 when the firm was reorganized. He was never a member of the family firm nor was he gifted with the family penchant and ability for making money, or with their interest in it. An easygoing man who liked easygoing people, he loved fishing, liked tying his own flies, made his own fishing rods and treated them with respect and reverence. He liked to drink, liked to go on fishing and camping expeditions into the woods, would in fact have been quite content, his daughter Elizabeth once said, to spend his life in the woods.

He was a scholar, his daughter said, but if so that tendency didn't blend easily with formal training. The Killams were Methodists and they tended to go to Methodist Mount Allison University in Sackville, N.B. The university's records indicate that William was at its now-defunct Wesleyan Male (commercial) Academy in 1875-6, and that he graduated. They also indicate that he then enrolled at the university itself at the age of 19, but that he was around only for the one year. They don't show what happened to him but the family story is that he was expelled.

He was once described as a "pioneer drygoodsman" in a firm called Killam and Bailey, and for a time he ran a store owned by an aunt. He later worked in a textile mill started with Killam money. In 1895 he was listed in a town directory as a baggagemaster on the Dominion and Atlantic Railway, the line that linked Yarmouth with Halifax via the Annapolis Valley. He was, in short, in a business sense, never a successful man as other Killams were successful. But he was a likeable man and he obviously had his own appreciation of the character of success.

In January 1884, at the age of 27, he married Arabella Hunter (Belle) Cann, the attractive daughter of Captain Harvey Cann, a mariner who owned a ship at 21. They lived at first in a house just past the Protestant cemetery on the outskirts of town, and when someone asked William Killam what it was like to live next to the dead he said they were the finest neighbors any man ever had. When their first child was born there on July 23, 1885, the father told his wife he'd like to name him Izaak Walton after the renowned author of that fishing classic, *The Compleat Angler*. She said she didn't mind, so the boy was given the name that would elicit comment for the rest of his days. His sister Elizabeth, three years younger, said he always liked it, and was proud of it.

3

THE HUSTLER

The day before Izaak Walton Killam was born the local *Herald* put out its weekly edition. You can find it today in the pleasant county museum in Yarmouth, and it affords an intriguing look into the sort of environment he entered. There is a notable touch of interest in money in its columns, plus the tang of politics and shipping and the measured life of the Victorian era. It reflects the proximity to New England that is still there in Yarmouth and, with it, a feeling for Mother England and a concern for the 18-year-old experiment called Canada.

On its front page the *Herald* carried two stories about fortunes, and they were strangely prophetic. The first said a 104-year-old spinster had died and now "a $40,000,000 windfall, known as the Churchill Estate, located in England and Newfoundland, is the precious plum which five persons living in New York, Brooklyn and Boston are seeking to divide between them." When Izaak Walton Killam died his estate taxes would come to a bit better than that and the Prime Minister would refer to them as a "windfall." The second story, immediately below the first, was about the widow of the assassinated American President James Garfield and it was headed "Mrs. Garfield's Fortune." It said "The recent reports concerning Mrs. Garfield's endowment of the Garfield

21

hospital . . . have created some curiosity about the lady's financial condition." The widow of Izaak Walton Killam would give millions to a hospital and it would help stimulate curiosity about her financial condition.

On an inside page the concern with money struck a more drastic and partisan note. The editor reprinted a Halifax *Recorder* editorial under the heading "The Career of Madness." Sir John A. Macdonald's Tories, it said in lament, were taking Canada straight to the dogs. "Yesterday everyone believed the financial condition of this country to be about as bad as it could be . . . Thousands of thoughtful men had been profoundly agitated over the appearance of affairs." But now the government had brought in supplementary estimates which raised total federal spending for the fiscal year 1885-6 to $37,000,000. The annual figures had been rising steadily and "soon the expenditure, at present rates, will be at least *thirty-nine millions*. Heaven knows what is to become of us . . . Verily we may ask — whither are we drifting?"

Part of the explanation was that Izaak Walton Killam had been born at a decisive time in national history. The Riel Rebellion had just been crushed in the West, and the success of the troubled, partially finished Canadian Pacific Railway in getting the troops out there to fight had broken a political impasse over a government proposal to make one more loan to see it through. Within a year Nova Scotia would fight a provincial election partly on the issue of secession, would vote for it — and never do anything about it. The sort of opposition Thomas Killam had represented had grown too feeble. The die had been cast, and the great historic significance of 1885, the year of The Last Spike, was that the final barriers to the opening of the West had been removed, that a transcontinental Canada had finally taken distinct form.

The *Herald's* advertisements were as prophetic for Izaak Walton Killam as were some of its articles. They laid heavy stress on bodily ills — he and his wife would have their share — and the bottled medicinal boons available to those who had them. The "Successful manager of the LARGEST HOTEL ENTERPRISE in America" had "found the Ayer's Sarsaparilla was a sure cure for an obstinate disease" and recommended it highly. Rheumatism, liver disorders, gout, the effects of high living, salt rheum, sores, eruptions and all the various forms of blood diseases; Ayer's Sarsaparilla would lick them all. Hagyard's Yellow Oil cured rheumatism too, and Freeman's Worm Powders were "pleasant to take." Minard's Liniment, a Yarmouth product, was "the great internal and external remedy for man and beast." At 25 cents a bottle, it cured sciatica, neuralgia, cramps, bruises, colds, quinzy and many other things. Burdock Blood Bitters "act upon the bowels, liver, kidneys and the blood." And if none of these would work there were more.

Cook and Stoneman were selling parasols at "great reductions," GOSSAMERS REDUCED, ladies' hose at 17 cents. E.H. Dane had BOOTS AND SHOES CHEAP. McLaughlin Brothers boasted that their "celebrated Princess Ida Corsets" were the "best value ever offered." Moses & Ross were plugging new prints, new sateens, new ginghams; Chute, Hall & Co. "popular new style organs, THE PARLOR GEM," Ewen & Company hammocks and croquet — "four ball setts, six ball setts, eight ball setts," Sheldon Lewis & Co. "the genuine mason jar" for preserving, Burrell-Johnson Iron Co. the Garfield Range, good for wood and hard or soft coal, "beautiful in appearance, perfection in operation." The Western Counties Railway (Yarmouth to Digby) urged people to remember the run out to Weymouth for the Milton Baptist Sunday School picnic; adults 75 cents, children 35. Thomas Killam, secretary, announced the annual meeting of the Yarmouth Duck & Yarn Co. (Limited). John Killam sought agents to sell "the History of the late Rebellion in the North West. Strike while the iron is hot." William Burrill & Co. of nearby Milton announced that they had become agents for the Leonard hay-mowing machine. W.H. Leonard, Jr., "inventor and manufacturer," touted his new "perfection creamer." Chandler Robbins announced an auction of "All of the grass on the Robbins Farm at Cheboque Point. A very superior crop." From Saint John, N.B., across the Bay of Fundy, C.H. Peters offered pressed hay, oats, middlings, shorts and other feed at "special low prices." Waterous of Brantford, Ont., advertised portable sawmills.

Lawyers, doctors, real estate agents, money-lenders, milliners, piano and organ tuners, hotels — they all had services to offer. So did Yarmouth & Boston Steamship Line whose steamer *Alpha* sailed every Wednesday evening for Boston, "after the arrival of the train from Digby," and left Boston every Saturday at noon to return. In competition, L.E. Baker's Yarmouth Steamship Co. urged people to take its *Dominion* to Boston on the "shortest sea voyage between Nova Scotia and the United States." It left Saturday, returned Tuesday.

The regular shipping "intelligence" column told of the comings and goings of these ships and of many others. It covered movements not only to and from Yarmouth but for other Nova Scotian ports and ports abroad. From cities in Britain, Holland, the United States and Germany, ship brokers, commission merchants and insurance agents, stevedore companies inserted notices that they were ready to serve those whose ships came their way. Shipping was still big news in Yarmouth. But in truth the peak had passed.

The years of growth had reached their climax in 1879 and the trend had been downward ever since — and the trend would continue. From a record 297 vessels in 1879, Yarmouth's registry had dropped to 225 in 1884, fewer than in 1867, the year of Confederation. And losses at sea had been worse than ever, so great indeed that Murray Lawson had decided that he must update his 1876 *Record of the Yarmouth Shipping* sooner than he had planned. In his new volume, *Yarmouth Shipping 1876-1884*, he said the death toll had been unprecedented. In 1879 alone a record 31 vessels had vanished, taking 106 human beings with them. Since 1875, 132 vessels had gone down, raising the grand total to 726.

The wooden vessels that had made Yarmouth prosperous were gradually being crowded off the more lucrative trade routes. Wrote Lawson in 1884: "It is not within the province of our present undertaking to trace the causes or probable results of the changes now going on in the commercial world by which iron and steam vessels are gradually supplanting their rival wooden sailing ships . . . But such is undoubtedly the fact, and wooden ships, for so many years the favorite investment of Yarmouth capitalists, are finding the task of obtaining profitable business growing yearly more and more difficult. Already the Pacific trade has

24

become the principal theatre of Yarmouth shipping operations . . . Her ships are gradually leaving the old Atlantic routes for voyages to the Far East, Java, China, India and California."

By 1897, when Izaak Walton Killam was 12 years old, the Yarmouth newspapers would finally drop that annual list of local shipping "which had been a leading and interesting feature since 1832." By the time of the celebration of the town's 150th anniversary, in 1911, the once large fleet was only a memory.

There was a tendency among Maritimers to blame all this on Confederation. The 1911 souvenir booklet was more realistic. It attributed the decline to "changes in economic conditions due to cables, telegraphs, foreign bounties, the opening of the Suez Canal, the cessation of European wars and the genesis of the 'ocean tramp.' "

But ships there still were in Izaak Walton Killam's youth, and widows and children of men lost on ships listed as "never heard of" after they vanished, and tales of the sea told by men who had known her at her best and at her worst. One of the places they liked to gather was around the pot-bellied stove in Killam Brothers' office. On its walls in the 1980s there was a mock plaque granting one Captain E.E. Manning membership in "Local 1000 retired shipmasters and sea yarns (truthful but mostly otherwise) union," and entitling him to Chair No. 1. He died in 1959 at the age of 95.

The things Yarmouth people long remembered best about the boy Izaak Walton Killam as he grew up in this atmosphere were that he was a loner and that he had a one-track mind about money. He didn't play baseball. He didn't play hockey. He did play a bit of tennis. One woman said he'd once had a crush on her mother, but others said he wasn't much for girls. He didn't chum around with boys much either. He went his own way, a withdrawn, quiet, pale, tall and gangling boy who was, several people said, neither popular nor unpopular.

His sister Elizabeth said in later life that he liked the beauty of the outdoors, that his cousin Lawrence, Frank's boy, and another cousin were friends of his, and they used to harness a donkey to a cart and go out on fishing trips. They would take a tent and go on to camp out after taking the donkey as far as the cart could go. Once the donkey vanished and they had to walk home. Once they came home soaking wet but happy.

Dr. Harvey Crowell had a more typical Yarmouth memory of the boy: a bright spring morning in 1898 when he came out to the Crowell home in Chegoggin. Harvey's brother Seth was in the same grade at Yarmouth Academy and apparently had confided that there were good trout-fishing brooks out that way. When the boy got there he had his fishing rod and gear strapped to his bicycle, and he was alone. He always liked fishing, his sister said, just as he liked his fisherman's name.

He was sent away to a private school, the Acacia Villa School in Horton's Landing, Nova Scotia, for a time but he didn't like it. Elizabeth Killam Rodgers recalled him saying that if his parents didn't take him out of there he'd run away. So they brought him home and he went to Yarmouth Academy.

That school was destroyed by fire years later so there are no records of his achievements, but the thing many people remembered was that he had a way with mathematics; he could figure very fast. His sister said mathematical skill was a Killam family trait, that her father was good at figures too and so were others, but her recollection was that her brother did well at everything, in fact led his class.   This recollection was reinforced by a 1927 news story which said he led his class and which included a statement by W.F. Kempton, a one-time Supervisor of Yarmouth schools, a mathematics teacher whom the boy liked and respected. Kempton remembered Izaak Walton Killam as "a pupil of marked brilliancy, a clever student in all studies and particularly given to originality." Still keen in his 90s, the memory of H.J. Wyman didn't quite agree. A teacher who also eventually became head of town schools, he said, yes, that the boy was good at math but wasn't interested in or much good at other things. Nor, Wyman said, had he ever expected him to amount to much in life; he just didn't have the aptitude for sociability that would help him on his way.

Certainly he was different, sombre and serious. A cousin, in her 90s, recalled him selling newspapers on a street corner, wearing short pants, boots and a cap, as boys did then, and a man coming up and offering him a nickel if he'd smile. He had his mother's big brown eyes, dark hair parted in the middle, an aquiline nose, large ears, and he always, said his sister, had his eye out for some project, "something exciting." He wasn't interested in work just for the sake of work, in jobs such as mowing the lawn for nothing. He wanted to make money. He was "a hustler," said a man five years younger who recalled young Killam working in his family's stationery store at Christmas time. He tried selling various things but by the time he was 12 or 13 he saw newspapers as his answer.

Dailies used to come into Yarmouth — which had three or four weeklies of its own — in two ways in those days: the Halifax and Saint John papers on the train from the Annapolis Valley, and, in summer, American papers by steamship from Boston. And, once in the business of selling them, young Killam eventually took measures which showed how things were going to be with him. He cornered the market. He got in touch with the publishers of the papers and lined up franchises to handle them. By the time Harvey Crowell's family moved into town from Chegoggin in 1900, the 15-year-old Killam had both the *Herald* and the *Chronicle* sewed up from Halifax and the *Telegraph* from Saint John. He also got franchises to handle the Boston and New York papers.

One published story said he slipped away to Boston on his own and came back with the *Globe, Post* and *Herald* all lined up. However he did it, he made the deal and his sister said the first his parents knew of it was when he announced one day he had to go down to meet the Boston boat. They were surprised and aghast, she said, at what he'd taken on.

Among some boys there was another reaction. They liked to bully him, tease him, taunt him, sometimes beat him up. On occasion, when he was at the railway station waiting for his papers, they would let the air out of his bicycle tires or loosen the handlebars or remove the chain. There is one story that, as he came back downtown with his bicycle out of commission, a woman asked if he'd had some trouble. He said yes, he had, but would she like to buy a paper? He rented space in a Main Street fruit store and worked from there, with the Post Office corner as the main base for operations because people came there to get their mail after work. "It was in the handling of these papers," wrote a Toronto *Daily Star* reporter in 1927, "that his keenness for financing was first observed. He went into the business as a vendor of newspapers on a rather extensive scale and, in so doing, he corralled a goodly number of boys and had them selling papers for him. He was, it might be said, a born leader . . . He handled the papers and did all the business while the boys he engaged were ready to fall into line with any proposal he saw fit to offer. In all his dealings with the others boys he was most honorable and all his associates put the utmost confidence in him."

Harvey Crowell, destined to be a prominent Halifax accountant and chairman of the board of governors of Acadia University, became part of the distribution system and got, as he recalled, one-half a cent as his share on a two-cent paper. The Halifax and Saint John papers, he said, were thrown out on the railway station platform in bundles even before the passengers got off. This was generally around five o'clock in the afternoon but it was often much later, depending on the arrival of the Saint John-Digby boat and, in winter, on snow in the Valley. The boys carried the bundles of papers into town or sometimes they'd jump on the trunk racks of the horse-drawn coaches that carried passengers. Killam would ride along on his bike. He eventually let Harvey Crowell have the Post Office corner for sales, and later he turned over the Saint John paper to him exclusively.

When the American papers came in by boat, the boys would be down to get them, too, and after helping the passengers carry their baggage across the wharf to the train waiting to head up the Valley they'd start to sell. The boats would be crowded with schoolteachers, businessmen and others bound for Halifax or up the Valley to see the Evangeline country Longfellow had made famous. By the time they opened the carefully-folded papers, they might see that they had already read them, but they were out of town by then. It was always best in summer, Harvey Crowell said, what with tourist tips and all.

Each night, when the papers were gone, he'd head for the Killam house to settle up. He always found his boss a squareshooter, Crowell said, but he'd ask an awful lot of questions, even in answer to questions. "He would ask you 50 questions in 10 minutes. He didn't tell you anything. He asked you questions. And he was always thinking about things. He was an exceptional thinker. He was studying then, but not just in school. He was an unusually different person, but he knew what he was doing." He could always see a way to make a dollar and he always had his eye out for good, reliable boys to work for him.

Yarmouth was a good place to sell papers, a busy place, in those days, even if its shipping was in steady decline. All winter, said Harvey Crowell, the new Grand Hotel would be filled with lobster buyers, men who carried $10,000 in their hip pockets and daily drove out to the wharves in outlying areas. The Grand, with its four storeys and great verandah, boasted that it was "The Largest and Finest Hotel in the Maritime Provinces," and some people said they figured there was no finer in all Canada. It was formally opened one night in July 1894, when Killam was nine, with a reception and ball which combined, said one account, to produce "the most brilliant social event ever attempted in Yarmouth. Under the radiant electric lights the scene was enchanting." People came to the party along asphalt sidewalks that had recently been laid along both sides of Main Street, at a cost of 35 1/2¢ a foot, or they may have used the Yarmouth street railway whose tramcars had been carrying passengers for two years on the first electric road in the Maritimes.

Electric street lights had first been installed in 1887, "five in number, on poles 40 feet high," and a large number of stores took out their kerosene lamps then too. But when this happened the past fought back. When the gas street lights, in since 1871, were "plugged, lanterns, etc., removed by order of the Light Committee . . . litigation followed."

The tall, skinny boy grew up amidst all this. He was only weeks old when Gunner Charles Porter came home from "active service in the Riel Rebellion" and was greeted by large crowds at the railway station. He was five when the town was incorporated. He was six when the "missing (rail) link" between Annapolis and Digby was completed in 1891 and Yarmouth for the first time "was placed in direct mail communication with Halifax and the rest of the continent"; nine when the Governor General and his lady, Lord and Lady

Aberdeen, arrived to be greeted by "an immense concourse of citizens who, headed by a torchlight procession, the Yarmouth Brass Band and Yarmouth Garrison Artillery, escorted them to the Grand Hotel"; nine when the steamer *Bowden* came in twice from Baltimore, Md., with supplies to build the South Shore Railway: mules, horses, wagons, wheel scrapers, carts, blacksmiths' outfits, plows, and "about 100 labourers (mostly colored)"; 12 when a public holiday celebrated the opening of the railway between Yarmouth and Pubnico, and the Grand Hotel was "literally covered with bunting"; 13 when the rendition of "Olla Podrida" was given at the Royal Opera House under the Auspices of the Old Ladies Home; 14 when a Yarmouth man imported from Boston the first motor carriage seen in Nova Scotia "and possibly in the Maritime Provinces"; 15 when Yarmouth's own veterans came home from the Boer War to be greeted with enthusiastic and generous civic receptions.

In later life there was sometimes a tendency to picture him as rising from rags to riches out of this small-town environment. It wasn't really that way. Certainly he lived in a town where other Killams were more well-to-do and prominent than his own branch of the family. There was a Killam on the board of the Bank of Yarmouth when it was founded in 1865, a Killam on the board of the Exchange Bank of Yarmouth when it was established in 1869, a Killam on the board of the Western Counties Railway Co. when it was incorporated in 1870, a Killam on the board of the Yarmouth Telephone Co. when it was set up in 1882, two Killams on the board of the Yarmouth Duck and Yarn Co. when it was incorporated in 1883, a Killam on the board of the Cooperative Deposit and Loan Society of Yarmouth when it emerged in 1885, and so it went. The simple fact was, in one woman's words, that the Killams were "money-makers." The boy's father never was but the fact remains that William Killam inherited money from his father, that his wife came from a good family, that she was a woman who liked to dress fashionably, and did, and who, it is said, yearned for better things, perhaps in doing so helping to shape the drives that motivated her son. When they moved into town to settle at the corner of Cumberland and Williams streets they lived in a home that is impressive to this day. The boy never went to college — few boys did in those days — but the family did send him to private school for a time and sent both his sisters, Elizabeth and Constance, to one too.

Then, when the boy was 16, his father died at the age of 45, and he became the male head of the family. He took the role seriously from the beginning. Having finished school, he went to work in the Union Bank of Halifax which had established a branch in Yarmouth. He already knew something about banks. He'd gone into one once with 50 cents to deposit. When the teller said they only took deposits of a dollar and up, he went out, borrowed 50 cents, deposited his dollar, then drew out half of it and repaid the loan. It was characteristic; he always had his own way of doing things.

The Union Bank hired him as a sort of clerk-office boy and his duties included keeping the premises clean, feeding the coal stove, keeping the cash books and ledgers. The branch was on Main Street, at the corner of Collins, and sometimes, it was said, he would go in after regular hours, snap on the lights and pace up and down beside the long customer counter, his head down, hands behind his back, lost in thought.

It was a scene that brought more taunts; boys, peering in through the windows at this spectacle of concentration, found new reason, as one put it years later, "to kid the daylights of him; you'd think he had the burden of the whole damned bank on his shoulders."

So the thoughts he took away from these hometown years were mixed thoughts. The taunting, the bullying, undoubtedly left its mark; a cousin said it could be pretty merciless. Perhaps also there was a feeling that, for various reasons, his branch of the family sometimes considered itself highhatted. The details don't matter too much. The key thing is that Izaak Walton Killam had some good memories of Yarmouth and that he had bad ones, and the bad ones were pronounced enough that when he became rich he refused to do anything for the place. So some of the town's memories of him, in turn, were shaped and shadowed by that fact.

4

"OH MY GOODNESS, HOW HE WORKED"

He was 18 when he left Yarmouth, and he was already known in town as a boy who could add numbers five at a time, who had no need to use the bank's interest tables because figures were a disciplined army in his head.

J.C. (Jack) MacKeen, a prominent Halifax businessman who got to know him as well as any man probably ever did, used to tell the story of his departure. He said Killam had told it to him. The boy was by nature, he said, "a bit of a procrastinator" and he tended to let some of his chores go, "let the entries in the ledgers, the cleaning, polishing and other duties accumulate to the point that they became oppressive to him. Thereupon, with a sudden burst of energy, he would go back after the day's work was done, complete all the entries in his books and by dint of manual labour make the office sparkle and shine to an impressive degree. It so happened that upon a certain night the general manager of his bank visited Yarmouth, unannounced, and after supper decided to take a walk down past the Union Bank. Glancing through the window, he saw a young man studiously engaged in completing his books, in extra tidy form, and the premises were as neat and clean as could be desired. Knocking on the door, he made an inspection of the office, checked the books, enquired the young man's name and went away with a mental note of young Killam's peculiar aptitude for a banking career. Shortly afterward Killam was transferred to head office."

It was in Halifax that he came into contact with the meteoric man who was to set him on the high road to success. Max Aitken, the later Lord Beaverbrook, had been raised in Newcastle, New Brunswick, as the son of a Presbyterian minister, and he hadn't amounted to much, by his own account, until his 21st birthday. Then, as a "feckless insurance agent," he'd gone on a three-day fishing party to a lake near Truro, N.S., heard a young Nova Scotian native talk of his hopes and plans for success in the United States, and experienced a profound conversion: "I never loafed again." Canadian business has seldom seen the equivalent of the explosion of enterprise that followed within the decade.

Aitken went from the insurance business into the sale of bonds and shares, then branched out under the patronage of John F. Stairs, a leading Halifax businessman who, in Aitken's words, "made me." Wrote Aitken: "Promoting and reorganizing Joint Stock Companies now opened out to me. Amalgamation of two banks was my first success. The sale of the Commercial Bank of Windsor to the Union Bank of Halifax (now merged in the Royal Bank of Canada) brought me a reward of $10,000. That was in the spring of 1902." He put the money into the formation of a new company, known as Royal Securities. It was incorporated in Halifax on April 18, 1903, to raise money for projects such as the Nova Scotia Steel & Coal Company in Cape Breton. There were no investment houses available for raising capital locally, so a group of Halifax men had started one. The minutes of the first directors' meeting were penned by Aitken, as "secretary pro-tem," and they are still in existence as a neat, one-page handwritten account.

Aitken once said that, in reality, "Royal Securities was me," but he needed help in the day-to-day operations of the business. There are various stories of how he found it in the person of Izaak Walton Killam. One is that he followed up a lead he got when he went to Yarmouth on business and heard a local man eulogize a young man named Killam, already in Halifax. One is that John F. Stairs first spotted Killam's talents. J.C. MacKeen's story is that Aitken asked his banker to recommend someone to him and that the banker, even though he hated to lose him, "felt obliged to recommend young Killam." Aitken's own story was that he'd met the young man when he went to the Union Bank. "Each day when he accepted my deposit we exchanged conversation."

Whatever the background, Killam went to work for Royal Securities in 1904 as a salesman of securities at the age of 19. "He had a big head," Aitken recalled in later years, "and he was more than intelligent." His bank teller's salary had risen to $750 a year and MacKeen's story was that Aitken doubled it. Aitken's story was that "I gave him $3,000 a year on trial" — and soon discovered that he'd made a mistake by giving him too much money:

"When he joined me he also joined a club, perhaps the City Club, and devoted himself to the game of bridge. His card sense was admirable. Afternoon and evening and often quite late at night he sat at the card table, indifferent to the call of our exciting ventures into the money markets of Eastern Canada.

"When the engagement of one year came to an end I reduced his salary to $1,500 with a percentage of our profits. A change came over him the next day. The bridge table was forsaken; the Club life was forgotten. And when the next twelve months ran out Killam's share was more than double the original salary."

Not long after Killam was hired Aitken became president of the company and he took it not only into domestic business but also into international finance. "A new era of electric lighting and electric tramway construction was setting in. We began to investigate opportunities for organizing some of these undertakings . . . Thus it was that I emerged from the bond-selling era and entered upon a successful career of promotion and management of Joint Stock Companies engaged in public utilities."

Within a few years Aitken felt he had outgrown Halifax. In 1906 he moved Royal Securities' headquarters to Montreal's St. James Street, then the unquestioned financial heart of Canada. The upper crust of the country's largest city had grown wealthy in its more than two centuries and a half of history — on furs, on wood, on grain, on shipping, on railways, on the geography that gave it a strategic location on the St.

Lawrence River, on the commerce pulsing out of the hinterlands to the east, the north and, ever more increasingly, to the west. The West was wide open now. Immigrants had been flowing in by the tens of thousands. The national boom which had coincided with the election of Wilfrid Laurier's Liberals in 1896 was transforming the country. It still had only 5,000,000 people. It was still predominantly rural and agricultural, still not sure whether it was a British colony or something else, something not quite defineable but increasingly Canadian. It was economically immature, still had to look to London if it wanted to raise much capital. But it was industrializing and it was ripe for adroit financial minds, and at 27 Max Aitken had learned the intricacies of high finance in a tough school. Many years after his arrival, Montrealers would still tell stories of the dramatic impact of his coming. And at his side came the 21-year-old Izaak Walton Killam.

Just what role Killam played in Aitken's explosion of enterprise it is impossible now to say, but there are some indications. Aitken himself wrote: "He was not only my first employee, he became my closest friend." He found Killam "truthful, upright in conduct . . . and indispensable." A Toronto *Daily Star* writer said Aitken's own "impetuosity was counterbalanced by the younger man's reserve, and Killam found in his brilliant leader a star to which his wagon might be hitched with alluring prospects for the future." J.C. MacKeen, himself long a Royal Securities executive, said Aitken "absorbed most of the limelight in the combination, but a great deal of the real and constructive thinking and development work was done by his junior partner."

The two worked together for a number of years which took them through what Aitken called "the most exciting era in Canadian industry" up to that time, years which taught them both where opportunities lay and where pitfalls threatened. Aitken, as an example, bought control of a trust company in 1906, then sold it a year or so later at a 50% profit. He had seen the ravages of a 1907 recession and had decided against managing other people's money. He freed himself "to follow my chosen path of providing finance for industry." It was a decision Killam would follow to the letter.

Royal Securities opened offices in London, Toronto, Ottawa, Quebec and Saint John, started the Montreal Engineering Company as a subsidiary for the management of public utility undertakings. It opened up vistas in power development and pulp and paper which were to be the pillars of Killam's later experience. Calgary Power Company was launched. Western Canada Power was started with the building of a hydro-electric plant in British Columbia; eventually it was taken over by the B.C. Electric Company at a handsome profit. In London, in 1910, the firm conducted the first large public financing in connection with the development of the Canadian newsprint industry, the placement of £1,000,000 worth of 5% first mortgage bonds of Price Brothers & Co. Ltd. to finance a new mill.

But above all Aitken is remembered in Montreal, sometimes bitterly, for his promotion of mergers of a number of small companies into a few big ones: the Canada Cement Company, the Steel Company of Canada, the Canadian Car and Foundry Company. Then in 1910 he went to England on a trip, and he didn't come back. He settled there, and he began that career in British politics and journalism which made him a knight, a peer, and a highly controversial figure.

The young Killam learned many lessons under Aitken, and he grew in stature and ability in doing so. For a few months in 1909 he broke away and set up his own investment business in Quebec City, but he returned to Royal Securities that same year. He was made managing director and went to London for four years to run its business there. He came back in 1913 to direct the firm in Canada, and in 1915, at the age of 30, he became its president. Four years later he arranged to buy Aitken out, to take control with a fellow Maritimer, Ward Pitfield, as a partner with considerably fewer shares. But really, colleagues said, Royal Securities was his to run from the time Aitken moved to London. Its founder had discovered new interests, new horizons.

Royal Securities had come into being, in the words of a booklet it put out in 1963, at a time of "superlative opportunities for the investment of capital. While agriculture, forestry and water power were seen as the principal basis of economic development, few could have foreseen the extent and variety of the rich mineral resources then lying underground and undiscovered — railways, municipalities, industries and services burgeoned on the flow of money readily available, particularly from the London market." It became, in Beaverbrook's words, possibly "the most vital and important finance house in Canada, and certainly the greatest money maker."

It was not an easy company to define. Finance house, investment house, merchant bank — men used them all to describe it. It was, in effect, an instrument for the implementation of the designs of the men who ran it. If Max Aitken had felt justified in saying that "Royal Securities was me," Izaak Walton Killam soon could have too. If Aitken had learned that his forte was "my chosen path to providing finance for industry," Killam had learned that too. That was the path he followed, and in its contours the company was shaped. It changed over the years, as Killam himself changed, but it was a long and very gradual process. "For a long time," as one Royal Securities man put it, "Killam wasn't much interested in investments in which he wasn't personally concerned." As one financial analyst saw it, in looking back years later, the firm was long "a personal, one-man investment house of a sort it would be hard for anyone to conceive of today." It was largely Killam's vehicle for investments in the industries of Canada and elsewhere, just as the subsidiary Montreal Engineering was a vehicle for carrying out and supervising the projects he conceived.

He lived and worked, in his early years in Montreal, in a financial milieu quite different from what it later became. Little has been written about it, as one man put it, because little was said. "You didn't tell anyone anything. You didn't spread your knowledge around. Everybody was secretive." Even prospectuses, those circulars designed to woo public investment, said little, and there were no governmental regulations that decreed that they should say more. "It was," recalled a financial analyst, "a pretty loose world."

St. James Street, "The Street" to insiders, was a realm unto itself, a few blocks of gray stone buildings east of Victoria Square, a place devoted to the handling of money through banks, brokerage firms, investment houses. It dominated

37

Canadian finance when Killam came there and it dominated for years thereafter. It had its own multitudinous links with the industries and businesses it fed with money, and made money from. It had its own tools of trade — loans, bonds, preferred shares, common shares, debentures, cast upon the marketplace after long thought as to which best suited each time and occasion.

It was one of its axioms that the investment business embraced the quickest ways both to make and to lose money. You lost money if promotions went sour, if judgment wasn't sound, if timing was off or the market turned down. You made money in various ways, through commissions for handling securities, through bonuses of common stock thrown into deals as sweeteners and which could in time be worth a good deal, through getting into things cheap, eventually issuing bonds and paying them off through earnings. Beaverbrook, in *My Early Life*, told of one case in which, he said, Killam made some $4,000,000 without really putting up a penny. "Maybe," he wrote, "the shares he held with me in the consolidation of Cinema Exhibiting Companies in Great Britain gave him swifter results than he or I expected. His interest amounted to 200,529 shares. He never got around to paying me the purchase money until I had negotiated the sale of the entire business to Ostrer Brothers. Killam paid £200,529 for his interest. He sold for more than £1,000,000 and he realized this striking gain in a single season."

The Street as Killam knew it perched at the crossroads of Canadian wealth, yet in its personnel it was essentially a small-city phenomenon, the thin top layer of that part of Montreal that bore one core credential: it spoke English. In later years old men could recall what the world of Montreal's upper crust had been like in days when people had horses and went riding on the mountain, when even the rich put their butter on the window sill to keep it cool, when people travelled by horse and carriage, and a car parked at night on St. Catherine Street was ensured of a policeman's care and attention, when there was green grass for boys to play on where the Ritz Carlton Hotel now stands, when the *Star's* Lord Atholstan kept his chauffeur dressed like a British coachman. Socially, it was a world of private parties, colorful, splendid, repetitive, held in massive, comfortable homes on or near the slopes of Mount Royal.

38

It was a milieu that had received, decade after decade, infusions of fresh blood. It took some in. It excluded others. It absorbed those it wanted to absorb within a generation.

Izaak Walton Killam came to know this milieu in time, especially after he moved out of a boarding house on Dorchester Street and took a suite at the Ritz Carlton. He came in as part of one of the tributary phenomena in Montreal life, the chronic exodus of Maritimers seeking larger horizons. They were everywhere in Montreal in those days, in the banks, in other financial institutions, in education, in shipping companies, elsewhere.

Killam was never particularly comfortable in the Montreal social milieu. He said so himself, and there were explanations. In part it may have stemmed from his links with the controversial Aitken. In part it may have stemmed from Killam's own shy, reticent, difficult character, in part from business jealousies.

In his younger years he got to know some of the belles of the city but it was said years later that they weren't too anxious to dance with him. It became awkward because he had little or nothing to say, though friends say he did like night life, going out on the town. But social life was always secondary to him. He was primarily a worker. "He worked, that man," said a colleague, "Oh my goodness, how he worked."

5

AN IRONIC PROTEST

Killam was 29 when World War I came, and he tried to enlist.
He was rejected on health grounds, apparently because of a
tricky heart, so he threw the efforts of Royal Securities into the
patriotic but unfamiliar function of selling government war
loan bonds. He was glad to do it. He was less happy about the
way it was done. He said so openly, and there is both
prescience and irony in what he had to say. Prescience because
Killam urged somewhat the same sort of comprehensive
government financial policies that were to be adopted in World
War II. Irony because of his usual attitude to taxes. Irony
because this was perhaps the first time that he came to national
attention and that he did so in a most uncharacteristic way, by
sounding off publicly.

Even though at least one newspaper said he was
assailing something dear to the heart of St. James Street, he
attacked the government mainly for issuing tax-free Victory
Bonds. But he went beyond that. He argued that Ottawa
should have tried to pay as much as possible for the war as the
war itself progressed instead of piling up debts that would have
to be paid in future years — by war veterans as well as others.

A debtor country, used to looking to London and then
increasingly to New York for large amounts of capital, Canada
had edged gingerly into the enormous and unprecedented

problems of wartime finance. The government for some time made the tariff the foundation stone of its financial structure, fended off a business profits tax till 1916 though fortunes were being made on war orders, resisted an income tax till the summer of 1917. It did float a first domestic war loan in 1915 — and raised twice as much money as the $50,000,000 it sought. In the crisis summer of 1917 the first so-called Victory Loan was launched, sought $150,000,000 and got $400,000,000; a larger one was planned for 1918. But the government, fearing reaction to its new income tax, decided the interest on Victory Bonds would be free of tax.

Killam placed his views before Parliament, the press and the public in great detail in September 1917. In a 10-page letter to Finance Minister Sir Thomas White, he singled out the tax-free provision as crucial. "It is," he wrote, "with great reluctance, but with a deep sense of responsibility and with the strongest feeling of its grave importance, that I venture to protest against a policy which . . . should, I feel, be immediately abandoned as harmful and unsound. That the tax-exempt war bond is fundamentally injurious to the economic life of Canada, is the prevailing opinion of those competent to judge of its nature and effects."

Ottawa should, he argued, have imposed "a reasonably substantial income tax" at the outset of war. Now that the government had belatedly imposed such a tax, it was giving tax-exempt bonds an unequal value in the hands of different purchasers. It violated the "elementary principle that public offerings and securities should be made to all subscribers at the same price and on the same terms." It was undesirable that "the Government should issue any further bonds on terms that may be construed as an attempt to take unfair advantage of the limited financial knowledge of the great majority of the people of Canada who will be asked to subscribe for the bonds on patriotic grounds. Our national security must have the same value in the hands of every individual Canadian, no matter what may be the extent of his personal estate. The people of Canada desire a graduated income tax to be effectively enforced. Continuation of the issue of tax-exempt bonds is calculated to nullify the graduated income tax. This matter is too serious to brook silence or delay."

41

Killam estimated that tax exemption meant for some well-off people a total return of 10 to 15% on government securities and he argued that "industrial and agricultural development will be checked and suppressed very materially." This "millstone" must be removed.

"It was and is clearly the duty of the Government to ensure that those who remain at home and participate in the benefits of the great increase in our national wealth . . . provide and extinguish in liberal measure, from current revenue, a most substantial part of the constantly increasing cost of carrying on the war . . . The provision for war expenditure from the incomes of our people has to date been far too small and must be increased, not only in justice to our army, but as a necessary measure for the protection of the future economic welfare of our whole people."

Killam argued that earlier long-term, non-callable, tax-free government bonds would provoke difficulties in postwar financing and that another issue would make "the position incomparably more difficult of remedy. If tax-exemption be firmly dealt with now, the situation in respect to our forthcoming and all future loans will be clarified instead of remaining clouded and obscure . . . Tax-exemption is wrong. Two wrongs have never made a right. There is only one remedy for wrong, and that is to correct it. The cost of correction is small; consequences of procrastination will be very great. All that is needed is courage and confidence on the part of the Government — courage to face the realities of the situation and confidence in the patriotism of the people."

With a copy of his letter to White, he sent a four-page letter to Prime Minister Sir Robert Borden, deprecating the inadequacies of Canada's war finance. It had, he said, not measured up to the country's efforts to produce munitions and food or to "the matchless achievements" of its troops. Despite the urging of "experienced financial authorities, no sound and comprehensive scheme of taxation had been introduced and the results obtained have been in keeping with the policy pursued." The government had harvested much less from ordinary revenues "than has been expended by the Canadian people for pleasure automobiles." Until 1917 appeals for an income tax "to meet the financial necessities of the state" had been in vain. Then one had only been imposed reluctantly and it still had not become "an effective source of revenue." A business profits war tax had been imposed but it "is perhaps not the least complaint of the commercial community that this tax has not been collected except where the willingness and anxiety of the citizen to pay has been greater than the zeal and industry of the Finance Department to collect."

Killam reviewed the government's various sources of revenue and concluded that it was apparent that "reliance must be placed upon the income tax, not only to defray a portion of our war expenditures and to meet the charges of our national debt, but in the future to maintain our very existence as a solvent state."

Because the government had failed to provide sufficient revenues to "defray out of current income a fair and adequate proportion of our vast war expenditures" it had turned to borrowing. By doing so "we have placed upon the returning citizen soldier . . . a burden of taxation that in operation involves his being called upon to pay an undue share not only for the uniform he has worn and the food he has consumed, but for the very ammunition he has used in the destruction of the enemy."

War bonds had been marketed at high interest rates and tax exemption had brought inequalities. "No sale of national securities should be made on terms that will result in exempting from taxation the income derived from accumulated wealth while placing a proportionately increased burden upon the earnings of industry and labour of the people." Tax-free securities meant that the man who made $1,000,000 out of war industry and invested it in them would be relieved of the payment of taxes on $55,000 per year of income while the war veteran "will during the period of readjustment at least earn a scanty livelihood out of which he must pay, perhaps not income taxes, because his earnings will be so small as to be exempt, but the proportion of the increased taxation in other forms which the exemptions of the income derived from tax-free Victory Bonds in the hands of the war-made millionaires will thus impose on him." The inevitable result would be "a not unreasonable demand on the part of our returned men to be relieved for life from the payment of all income taxes."

43

Killam said he was "confident that it does not require tax-exemption to induce Canadians to lend their money to the nation for war purposes. The rich have not asked for such a concession. The average citizen has not even concerned himself to ascertain what tax-exemption means." Canadians were willing to do their bit, on a fair basis. But tax-free bonds were unsound, extravagant and unfair.

A copy of that letter also was sent to the press and Members of Parliament, and it brought from Borden a brief but pointed reply. He wrote that he understood that White had already answered. "In any case," he added, "since you state that you have already sent copies of your letter to the press and have otherwise circulated it, I conclude that it is not your chief object to elicit a reply from me."

In his reply, White wrote that war loan policy had received "the most careful and attentive consideration on the part of the Government in conjunction with the best financial opinion of Canada and in the light of the then prevailing market conditions. No country has been more successful in its war finance than Canada and the finances of no nation engaged in the war today are upon a better or more sound basis . . . I know positively and from personal experience that the making of our Victory Loan issues taxable would most seriously affect the amount of subscriptions unless a higher rate of interest were offered, and this we regard as inadvisable." The government could not "afford to take chances which may hinder success, by experimenting with new provisions as to taxation, the proceeds of which would be, from the standpoint of national revenue, of comparatively small importance."

When the Director of Public Information in Ottawa made a summary of press reactions to Killam's letters, he said they were "being published in a number of newspapers and are being freely commented upon." The Quebec *Chronicle*, he noted, had remarked that "if the Government's financial policy is as mischievous as Mr. Killam represents then Sir Thomas White has much to answer for, but if it is only a question of Dives grinding his own axe there will be little sympathy from the average man or from the large class of clerical workers who, unlike either organized Capital or organized Labour, have not shared in Canada's increased prosperity." The

44

Chronicle regretted the appearance of the letters because they were "quite as likely to kill the whole bond issue as to enable him (Killam) to carry his point."

The *Financial Post* regretted that the government "ever allowed itself to be drawn into its present undesirable position" which was the subject of "very general condemnation." The Montreal *Gazette* found Killam's logic "cogent and lucid," that "other things being equal, no peculiar privileges should be attached to government securities, especially when the privilege disturbs the basis of income taxation and imposes some ultimate difficulty in providing public revenues." Yet the money must be obtained and this was an overriding "primal consideration." Moreover, in tax exemption, the U.S. was doing what Canada was doing. From the Edmonton *Bulletin* came the opinion that "if a mistake was made it was in issuing the earlier bonds as non-taxable." Once that was done the government had lost the initiative. Toronto's *Mail and Empire* pointed out that leading American newspapers were supporting Washington in actions similar to those taken in Ottawa. The Toronto *Daily News* said Ottawa had cause for "self-congratulation in the fact that the American Government has adopted two of the outstanding features of Canada's war financing."

Any chance the issue had of being sustained ended with the collapse of the German armies and the Armistice of November 1918. But a postwar loan to help pay for the war was put on a taxable basis and the government in World War II made war loans taxable too. Just what Killam's motives were it is impossible to establish now, but men who knew him well later said they were convinced that he firmly believed that tax exemption favored the rich, that it was both wrong and unnecessary, that the government had underestimated the zeal of the Canadian people.

Graham Towers, first governor of the Bank of Canada, said many years after the event that he felt Killam was right and that later events proved him right. He was also convinced, from knowing Killam, that the letters were entirely sincere. As a financier and a wealthy man "it may have been an unusual thing for him to do, but then he was an unusual man."

There is one footnote to the whole thing. Killam's firm, like other investment houses, had handled the government war bonds without commission. When peace came Ottawa sent the company a cheque and an expression of gratitude for its efforts. Killam wouldn't cash the cheque. He had if framed.

6

DISASTER

When Killam was named to the board of Calgary Power in 1917, the *Montreal Star* cited it as "another instance of the rapid advance of the younger generation of financiers." By the end of the war, in the opinion of one prominent financier, he was recognized as "a leader of Canadian corporate finance." At 33, still single, he was a wealthy and a rising man. Moreover, the prospects for his kind had never seemed brighter. The war had demonstrated for the first time Canada's ability to raise large sums of money internally. In all, six war loan drives had raised $2.2 billions from a total of 2,285,171 subscriptions. Said a Royal Securities booklet: "It was an impressive contribution for a country of about 8,000,000 people, most of whom had no previous experience in buying investment securities. It can be said that the loans gave to Canadians their first great nation-wide lesson in saving and in the art of investment. The period of 1914-18, in fact, saw the birth of the 'Canadian' investment market."

The country stepped buoyantly out into the postwar world, and Killam bought Royal Securities and stepped out with it. Then within two years he ran head-on into disaster, into the Riordon debacle. A sensation at the time, it rocked financial circles and was remembered for years after as what one writer called "one of the tragedies of Canadian financial history."

The story is rooted in part in that growth of the pulp and paper industry which Killam singled out as one of his main approaches to success, and to some extent in the wartime transformation of Canadian thought. The industry was growing fast in the last quarter of the 19th century, but it was in the early years of the 20th that it really took off. A remarkable expansion stemmed from various factors. America's reckless exploitation of its forests was reducing its supply of pulpwood towards the famine level. Canada had the forests to meet that demand, and the cheap waterpower to turn trees into pulp and paper. By 1903 E.B. Biggar, founder of *Pulp and Paper Magazine*, was predicting that "Canada is destined to be the greatest pulp and paper manufacturing country in the world."

Government action on both sides of the border stimulated the dream. In Canada, early in the century, Ontario banned export to the U.S.A. of pulp cut on its Crown lands, and a gathering chorus urged that this be done elsewhere. The *Pulp and Paper Magazine* reported a growing feeling that an embargo should be put upon the export of pulpwood so that American paper manufacturers would be forced to put up mills in Canada. The pressure worked. In 1909, at a time when most of the industry was concentrated in the central provinces, Quebec announced that it was going to bar the export of pulpwood cut on Crown and unpatented lands. In the United States, pressures from newspaper publishers seeking cheaper newsprint helped stimulate an historic American offer of trade reciprocity, only to have Canadian voters reject it in 1911. But the publishers ended up with the duty-free newsprint imports they wanted anyway.

With these advantages, the industry grew "by leaps and bounds" right up to the war, despite a shortage of trained professionals. The war only made it grow faster, so much so that the *Pulp and Paper Magazine* kept warning against artificial expansion. In 1919, amid a world paper shortage, foreign buyers were offering an astronomical $150 a ton for paper that ordinarily sold for half as much.

Against this background, no company name loomed larger than that of one called Riordon. It had been associated with the industry since 1857 when John Riordon started in business in Brantford, Ont., as a trader in paper. In a long process of growth and expansion, the Riordon firm became, in the words of a magazine account, "pioneers in the manufacture of sulphite fibre" and "recognized as the leading pulp experts of the North American paper trade." In 1918 the company began to build at Temiskaming, Que., the so-called Kipawa mill that was designed to cash in on soaring demand for bleached sulphite pulp for the making of rayon and other products. It would tap forests containing black spruce, "the best in this continent for the manufacturing of pulp." By 1920, its first production unit had been rushed into operation.

In June of that year the *Pulp and Paper Magazine* carried a feature on the company that was aglow with optimism. Riordon's history, it said, "is one of the most important chapters in the industrial growth of Canada. Few industries have shown such rapid and steady progress during the past decade, and its maximum attainment is by no means yet in sight . . . The company is growing as Canada grows and always keeping in the van of progress."

With European production of pulp decreasing, with American consumption growing, there was "tremendous demand" for the Canadian product, and Riordon was in an excellent position to prosper. Then, after the article was begun, the writer said, there had come news of "a transaction of the greatest magnitude in the forest industries of Canada." The "great holdings and operations" of both W.C. Edwards & Co. Ltd. and Gilmour and Hughson Ltd., in the Gatineau Valley region, were being united with Riordon in a new company to be called Riordon Company Ltd. The company would own, control or lease "the greatest area of pine and pulpwood holdings in the world under one control." In addition, it would control "enormous natural storage areas" for development of power.

Killam was deeply involved in all this; Royal Securities had done business with Riordon for some time, and the time seemed to Killam and to others to be ripe to do more. Within the company itself, vice president Carl Riordon was all for the Kipawa project, and overrode the doubts of his father, Charles, the president. Carl Busch Thorne, an engineer, a patrician and a director of the company, provided decisive enthusiasm. In fact, said one writer, it was he who "convinced

49

Riordon to build the mill" and it was he who got the job of building it.

The time *did* seem ripe. There had been, said the *Canadian Annual Review*, "a tremendous rise" in pulp and paper stock values. There was during 1920 a "marked process of reorganization" of companies in the industry, of which the Riordon development was "the most important." Added the *Review*: "I. W. Killam and the Royal Securities Corporation of Montreal were instrumental in the creation of the Merger and the total interests involved were estimated at $60,000,000." On June 18 an issue of preferred shares, carrying a bonus of 20% common stock, was put on the market by the new company. It was taken up and a good block of shares sold in the United States.

A year later: calamity. The wartime and postwar boom vanished into the recession of 1921. It didn't last long, but it was felt deeply in many ways, not least in the pulp and paper business.

Riordon's big pulp operations were caught with "large inventories of high-cost supplies and bond issues and loans on which to pay interest." On the building site itself, the arrogant, self-confident Thorne — once described as a "Norwegian with a Prussian mentality" — made expense a secondary consideration as he rushed construction in an attempt to cash in on the booming market. Result: the value of Riordon securities plunged and its long-proud name became a synonym for disaster. A committee of directors reported in May that liabilities exceeded assets by some $3,700,000. It said the company's position was "due to commitments for construction and other expenditures having been undertaken before adequate financial arrangments were made — the construction expenditures on the Kipawa plant having exceeded the original estimate of cost — and to the world-wide reaction in general trade conditions." Unless $5,500,000 in working capital was obtained at once the business would not be able to continue even though "the soundness and value of your company is unquestioned." The key, said the committee, lay in shareholders putting up the required money by buying a new issue of mortgage and collateral trust bonds. It urged them to do so. It also asked creditors for a one-year extension on the payment of debts, and a meeting of creditors agreed to it. But the company's losses for the August-October period alone exceeded $1,000,000 and the attempts to get the shareholders to put up more money ran into trouble.

Amidst all this, the elderly Charles Riordon stepped down as president, his wealth savaged; son Carl took over. A new directorate was formed, with Killam as a member and a vice president. But it was common gossip on St. James Street that, at 36, he was finished. In Royal Securities itself, one man would recall, "things were a mess," salaries were cut and uncertainty spread. Yet — and this is one of a number of stories about Killam that may or may not be true — it was later said that at this dark hour he came up with a gesture of confidence and defiance: he bought a Rolls-Royce and had it parked in front of his office.

It was not, however, at his own office that he spent most of his time in those days. He was working hard elsewhere. "He was always at his best in a crisis," a colleague said. "He seemed to like nothing better than the opportunity to tackle a seemingly impossible financial problem — and solve it." This time, said another, "we didn't see much of Killam for weeks." He was at Riordon's Montreal headquarters trying to put things back together again. He knew Riordon had great intrinsic strength. He worked to develop some new method for putting behind its resources the financial support that would let the company survive.

The struggle went on for months, for years, and it developed in a classic corporate form. There were both bondholders and shareholders, and the bondholders had the prior claim on Riordon assets. There were two groups of them holding two different types of bond, but their protection committees cooperated to sponsor their claims.

It was Killam's apparent aim to find some way to protect shareholders to whom he had sold securities, and simultaneously to keep the company solvent and under Canadian control. In the wings stood America's International Paper Company, biggest in the world and hungry for expansion in Canada through its young subsidiary, Canadian International Paper. There were, said one published account, "many attempts to find a workable solution." Killam did come

51

very close to bringing it off at one stage at least, only to have certain interests pull out on him at the last minute. Finally it was necessary to admit defeat. The bondholders were freed in 1924 to put the company up for sale. The bond committees, the only bidders, got it for $7,300,000. Riordon bonds promptly took a swing upward as speculation grew as to what they would do with the firm. On July 4, the *Financial Post* said it was "logical" that International Paper should buy it: it had "already decided to spend many millions in Canada — and Riordon has extensive timber limits." By that time Riordon's mills were operating with the exception of one old one and "an operating profit is being earned that would be sufficient to meet fixed charges if there were not the necessity for building up working capital."

In March 1925 the expected happened: for $26,210,000 International bought "what once was Riordon." It soon announced that C.I.P. was going to build a huge newsprint mill on the Gatineau and that the Kipawa mill was to be expanded. In 1926 Kipawa was reported to be producing about half the world's supply of bleached sulphite pulp going into rayon, though it was only in that year that the first rayon-trade pulp was ready.

As the returned buoyancy of the '20s thrust on, International prospered on the design Killam had helped build. But the Riordon shareholders found themselves with nothing; there wasn't enough money from the sales to cover their investments. The shadow that lingered over the name of Royal Securities would make it difficult for Killam's salesmen to sell securities in some areas for years. What made the situation worse for him at the time was the fact that Riordon wasn't alone in damaging his fortunes. A firm called Canadian Connecticut Cotton in which he was involved fell on troubled times. He had also gone into Cuban sugar, a commodity whose price had been elevated to great heights by the war, then crashed disastrously.

Killam learned from these experiences. He became more conservative. He turned to other fields. He also learned lessons which, one suspects, were of real benefit to him in trying days ahead. Perhaps he also learned something about the crucial quality of timing. "His real trouble," said one financial man, "was that he was 20 years ahead of his time. His vision outdistanced what was practical." Canada wasn't ready for the scope of what he had in mind. If it had been, lamented one pulp and paper expert, the three or four other prominent Canadian companies in the field would have banded together to support Riordon, both to save it as a Canadian firm and to "establish a public image of pulp and paper solidarity for the lasting good of the whole industry."

7

A MARRIAGE AND

A COMEBACK

Perhaps the experience touched Killam in one other way. Riordon's fate was very much in question when he got married. He had met Dorothy Brooks Johnston when she came to Montreal for a visit with friends. Her own story was that she went to a party in Montreal society, saw this tall, shy, withdrawn man with the eyes of an owl, and promptly announced to a friend her intention to marry him. They were married at her brother's home in St. Louis on April 5, 1922. He was nearly 37 and she was 22, and she was destined to have a marked influence on him for the rest of his days.

Into his bachelor existence she introduced flair, style, the dramatic impulses of a born actress. It would be a good number of years before a reporter called her "a legend in her own right," but the impact was immediate. Proud of her American heritage, she had the strong competitive streak which often runs in the American character. It had made her a crack swimmer, so good that she had achieved Olympic standards. In Montreal, she impressed one new friend as "a dynamo" and was soon busy mastering other sports. She took up golf, and Killam told her he'd give her $100 if she broke 100 for 18 holes that season; she did it ahead of schedule by hounding professionals to correct her faults. She took up tennis and kept at experts till she was good at that too. She liked to play bridge, and she read books and took lessons to improve her game. She took up salmon fishing because Killam loved it, and she became an expert at casting a line. She was, in short, a perfectionist.

She was small and blonde and she had what people call "a lovely figure." She liked parties, and thanks to her the Killams led a considerable social life even though her husband could be quite content to sit for a long time without saying a word. One of the many tales told of him was that he once sat this way at a party, his thoughts obviously far away, then suddenly sat up, said "My God, I need a million dollars" and left. Dorothy was devoted to him but these silences could rile her. "Walton," she said as they drove home one night, "I could kill you." It didn't change him. At times, in fact, he would chide her for talking too much about things he felt she didn't know enough about. "If you have nothing to say," he'd say, "don't say anything."

At times they went with friends to a favorite Montreal night spot, the Mount Royal Hotel's Normandie Roof. She loved it. Killam was apt to slip away early. At one party she passed herself off as a recent arrival from Germany; she'd picked up the language while staying there as a young girl with an aunt who was fluent in German, held an academic appointment in philosophy at a German university, and was a friend of the royal family. Mrs. Killam liked to tell of the time she herself met Kaiser Wilhelm, on a morning when she was playing with his children and he dropped in.

She had, as the years went by, no children of her own though she did have at least one miscarriage. From the first she and her husband lived in a rambling, three-storey stone house on Montreal's fashionable Sherbrooke Street which Killam had bought earlier. There would be others in due course but this was where she entered his life at a dark corporate moment, bringing both a breath of fresh air and perhaps even a touch of good luck. For she was at his side in those years when he dug himself out of the most troubled phase of his career and, in retrospect, the impressive thing is how quickly and how well he did it.

His bride, it was said, wanted Killam "to cut a dashing figure" in the wake of Riordon. That wasn't his personal style.

55

But financially it became an apt description of what happened. Perhaps the most dramatic thing in his entire career is the fact that at least by 1927 — six years after Riordon's collapse, two years after its sale — he had made a comeback that was considered remarkable. He had made, it was said, a second fortune and Riordon was looked upon not so much from the standpoint of the disaster itself as from the way he had rebuilt his name and possessions out of the shambles it had left. "He made a magnificent recovery," the *Toronto Daily Star* quoted an acquaintance as saying, "and his last five years have been years of uninterrupted success."

Said a *Star* writer: "What is claimed as the outstanding success of the financier's career is the recuperation of Royal Securities." There were many, he wrote, who saw Riordon as a failure but Killam's friends "claim that his judgment in backing the development has been amply vindicated by the fact that Riordon was bought up later by the International Paper Company and had progressed so far as to be capitalized probably more highly than ever Killam planned. He saw a great vision but he saw it at the wrong time, it is said. But its possibilities were there as its success under American exploitation has proved, and with his judgment thus vindicated Mr. Killam has also given proof of his recuperative ability by bringing back the Royal Securities Corporation into the forefront of Canadian banking institutions.

"This reputation for creativeness had been won by achievements of a truly constructive kind and there are many Canadian and other industries which he brought to the attention of Canadian investors. All of his big ventures with the exception of Riordon were successful."

In another 1927 story the *Star* said "No greater tribute to the strength of character of this exceptional young Canadian could be produced than the fact that . . . Mr. Killam has, by hard work, intense concentration and an energy which has won the admiration even of his opponents in the financial world, completely re-established his fortunes and brought himself again to the forefront of Canadian affairs. A prominent Montreal stockbroker said this about him in an interview: 'Walton Killam is a great man and you will hear big things of him in the future. On the street, as in the prize ring, they do not often come back. Killam's remarkable recovery of a foremost position among Canadian men of finance is eloquent testimony to the exceptional qualities of his character.' "

It is difficult now to trace in much detail the story of how this comeback was achieved, just as it is difficult to chart in detail much of what he did throughout his career. He left no papers and, indeed, it is typical that this book has depended to an unusual degree on the memories of people who knew him and what he did. While libraries, archives, company, newspaper and magazine files were a very real assistance, it was these recollections which helped most of all. His records were largely destroyed in a 1969 fire at Royal Securities headquarters, and colleagues doubted that they would have cast much light on his activities anyway. He was just too secretive, and many of the key events never got put down on paper.

His comeback started, said colleagues, as a gradual process and then gathered momentum in the boom of the '20s. "He sent his staff out ringing doorbells. He went looking for things to do. He took whatever offered." In the back of his mind, said one man, "was the thought that a lot of people had lost a lot of money through Riordon and that he'd try to help get it back." He got into real estate, financed apartment buildings like Sherbrooke Street's great, gray Chateau. He financed grain and elevator companies in the West. In one major coup, he turned his nemesis, the crash of 1921, into a golden advantage. After the depression sent the six-year-old Mattagami Pulp and Paper Co. into receivership, he bought some millions of dollars worth of its debentures cheap, got effective control of the company and then sold it profitably in 1926.

Assailed in Canada, he turned some of his attention elsewhere. He had taken over Cuba's Camaguay Electric Co., a public utilities concern, in his purchase of Royal Securities from Beaverbrook. With an American engineer named Carl Giles in charge, it was built into a substantial business, so substantial that an American company eventually wanted to buy it. Killam was told that he shouldn't sell, that the company was worth more than was offered, but in 1926 he did sell at a substantial profit. Beaverbrook later said Killam had paid him $55 a share and sold them for $250, for a total of $2,500,000.

He apparently wanted the money to do other things in the Caribbean and Latin America, in the area for which a number of his grandfather's ships had been named. In 1926 he organized a new holding company called International Power and embarked upon a program of modernization and expansion of companies he bought or already owned. He became locked in a race with an American company called Ebasco — Electric Bond and Share Co. — in development of the area around the old Spanish Main.

With Montreal Engineering as his tool for construction projects, he took subsidiaries of his new company into production of power for the tin of Bolivia, the oil of Venezuela. He bought the obsolete Bolivian Power Co. from French interests, and got the municipal lighting contract it had for La Paz. The French had been paid in local currencies, but they had had difficulties in getting the Bolivian government to pay at all for its share of the electricity. Killam's company struck a bargain with the government to wipe out the old debts if it were paid in future in U.S. dollars or Swiss francs. It used these currencies to modernize, to bring in new power-generating equipment. It surveyed the Andes for power sites, got a contract to service all tin production, then built plants and transmission lines to do the job. Some of Montreal Engineering's construction work in the mountains was said to be "remarkable."

In British Guiana, Killam inherited from Aitken's day a plant that burned wood to generate power. It was eventually converted to oil. He bought on the London market a lot of the stock of the Puerto Rico Railway, Light and Power Co. at a time when it was in financial difficulties. He got control and updated its facilities. He did much the same in Mexico when the Monterey Railway, Light and Power Co., a firm launched in 1905 by British and Canadian capital, fell $1,721,000 in debt to a Canadian bank. For $1,200,000 Killam's International Power Company acquired the position of the bank together with debenture stock and 35% of the voting stock. By 1930, two years later, he had bought up enough additional voting stock and senior securities to give him effective control of a firm which provided telephone, trolley bus, power, water and

58

sewage services. In his projects, he hired local labour but usually put Canadians or Americans in the key jobs. He would countenance no political payoffs. When his firms paid taxes, they got receipts.

He also was active in Canada. In British Columbia, Killam became involved in the fate of yet another victim of the depression of 1921, the Whalen Pulp and Paper Co. which had plants at Port Alice, near the northern tip of Vancouver Island, and on Howe Sound, some 30 miles north of Vancouver. In 1921 Whalen ran into trouble from a combination of economic decline and lack of practical experience in pulp manufacturing and marketing. The company went into receivership, and Killam became involved on behalf of the security holders.

There was scant interest in financial circles in a company in Whalen's position. Its plants weren't too good, said a Killam colleague; its stock was virtually worthless. But Killam recognized the potential value of its timber limits. He worked out a formula, it is said, which enabled the bondholders to recoup their investment and the shareholders to take their chances on eventual recovery. He himself ended up in control when a trust company put the company up for sale.

He reorganized the firm as British Columbia Pulp and Paper Co. Ltd., and hired his cousin and boyhood fishing friend Lawrence Killam to run it. Lawrence was a mechanical engineer, had been a university professor for some years, and had done work for some of Izaak Walton Killam's other companies. He had studied the Whalen properties for Royal Securities before they went into bankruptcy.

It was his original intention to spend only two or three years in the new job. But his cousin was impressed with the progress he made in restoring the company, in shipping pulp mainly to Japan, and he persuaded Lawrence to remain on. The time would come when Izaak Walton Killam would say his cousin had turned "a bunch of kindling wood into a pretty fair company."

Power was the common focus of a number of his other projects. Montreal Engineering's Geoffrey Gaherty was sent to Alberta to look over the potential of Calgary Power, a company that had been formed in 1910 but didn't seem to be going anywhere. Its stock had been kicking around the market, worth very little, but the expert came back to Montreal with a glowing report of the company's prospects. Killam liked what he heard and began buying up shares; he got control and began to expand the company under Gaherty's able direction.

By the mid '20s it was moving out from its Calgary base under a relatively major program of expansion designed to provide electricity for many of the rural communities in south and central Alberta. They had been mainly supplied by internal combustion engines, a service which produced power only on a part-time basis in many instances and then at high cost. Over a period of years Calgary Power gradually acquired their electric systems and bought up franchises. New transmission lines began to web out through the countryside from the main hydro plants on the Bow River. As demand grew, the company made plans to meet it. By 1927 construction of a 30,000 kilowatt plant, called the Ghost Development, on the Bow, some 30 miles west of Calgary, was commissioned, and financing was provided through long-term securities and bank loans. Two years later it was in operation.

At the same time Killam got into power in Ontario, formed the Ottawa Valley Power Co., and joined with Ontario Hydro in constructing a joint development at Chats Falls, Hydro building on the Ontario side, Killam's firm on the Quebec side. Hydro contracted to take all the power.

He looked farther east and saw opportunities there too. In Halifax a local power company had run into trouble after the war and had been bought by the Rockefeller interests in the United States. They were willing to sell, and in time Killam got effective control of Nova Scotia Light and Power. He got into power in New Brunswick and Prince Edward Island. In Newfoundland he took over a rundown little company, reformed it as Newfoundland Light and Power and made it part of the holdings of International Power.

Most of these cases were classic examples of Killam's goals and methods: he spotted potential, got in cheap and held on while he developed or expanded the business. He turned to his own advantage the ravages of the 1921 depression that had threatened to ruin him over Riordon. It made things cheap, and it cast up opportunity. He seized it. As one man put it, "he was always reaching out and he had a smell for things that very few men have, a great mind for knowing when to buy something." He wasn't interested in making quick profits from the things he bought. He was interested in building them up. He shared with Beaverbrook a belief that "It is best to buy and hold on. Moving in and out of the market is never as satisfactory." If any one thing was said of him repeatedly it was this: "He was a builder."

8

THE DREAMER

Gradually anecdotes and opinions and even sobriquets spun a web around his name. When people told stories of him after he was gone others might say they doubted that they were true or still others that they'd never heard them though they did seem to square with what they knew of Killam. So you were left, as you tried to pin together the story of his life, left with this thin mist of potential apocrypha drifting over the realities. Yet even if some of the tales were embellished that in itself said something about the way people saw Killam or thought of him.

It became part of his mystique that his skill in reviving firms in difficulties made him known as a "collector of antiques" and a "doctor of companies," and Harvey Crowell, his boyhood employee, had good reason to know the second of these was deserved. As an accountant, he went to Killam with a client whose business was in trouble. Killam listened, diagnosed the problem, suggested remedies. The man did what he suggested and, said Crowell, it worked.

Anecdotes threw light on his attitudes, his methods. Halifax lawyer Frank Covert remembered getting a call from him late one night, and Killam instructing him to then call someone else.

"But, Mr. Killam," said Covert, "it's after midnight."

"That's a good time to call," Killam said. "He'll have your message fresh in his mind when he wakes up."

It was said that he never took out insurance, that he didn't believe in it. It was said by C.H. Link, long head of Royal Securities publicity department, that Killam liked to play crap and poker and that he always seemed to win. Once, said Link, Killam came back from an ocean voyage and asked how the French franc was doing. Then he produced wads of francs won on the trip. Gordon Shirres recalled a day when he and other Royal Securities salesmen got their annual bonuses, repaired to a club and set up a crap game. Killam, he said, dropped by, got into the game and soon cleaned up. Then he gave the salesmen their money back and told them to go home and that he hoped they'd never gamble their bonuses again.

If you asked people to describe him, you got various answers. A financial writer remembered him as "a distant, unapproachable god," a senior broker as "a tremendous man," a colleague as "a rock of Gilbraltar." Critics remembered him as a tough competitor, in many ways a selfish, difficult man.

People used various words in trying to describe him: unique, quaint, exacting, extraordinary, an individualist. He was a big, broad-shouldered man, more than six feet tall, close to 200 pounds in weight, and many people were bewitched by the big, wide, deep brown eyes he had inherited from his mother. They were called owlish, piercing, penetrating, absorbing, dominating. "They seemed," as one acquaintance put it, "to look right through you."

Killam ran Royal Securities and its staff of roughly 300 in his own way. He largely left its day-to-day operations to others while he wove his financial designs. At annual banquets he spoke very briefly, let someone else preside. In the office he was, colleagues said, an aloof, lonewolf figure. It was said that he couldn't fire anyone personally, that he left that to others. But he had his own decimating way of handling people who had lost his confidence: he simply ignored them.

He was a spartan running what was known on The Street as a conservative house, one which years later a *Financial Post* writer would call "an old-line firm, an ornament of Canada's social history," a symbol of "probity and caution." To it, one colleague felt, he imparted something close to an "old-fashioned Maritime religious feeling," a rooted character.

He dressed conservatively in dark clothes from London, although this tendency became less pronounced under the influence of his wife. He had no expensive tastes apart from salmon fishing. He didn't like change. He didn't like to walk much either, almost invariably was driven to work. When he went on a trip, he would never hire a private railway car. He took a drawing room.

He rarely paid high salaries to his top men. It is one of the ironies of his life that a man destined to be called the richest person in Canada felt that too much money wasn't good for people. He did carry large quantities of stocks for key employees which ultimately made them very rich but he obliged them to pay interest on the loans he made to them to buy at reasonable rates.

He worked for some years in a small office on the ground floor of a gnarled, seven-storey, Victorian-era building at 244 St. James Street, one adorned with scrolls and carved oak panellings. He had a large old mahogany desk at which he worked, and behind him a roll-top desk on which he kept papers. They absorbed nearly all the available space, and they were seldom cluttered.

Royal Securities eventually bought the building and plans were made for an executive suite. It was suggested to Killam that he get a new desk but he said his old desk was perfectly all right. He took both old desks with him. They did get him some bookcases and a board table. No one could remember ever seeing more than a few things in the bookcases. The board table was seldom used. Killam didn't like big meetings. He liked to meet with only a few people at a time, and then he liked to listen and ask questions. Said a cohort: "Ask him a question and he was apt to ask you one, or turn the conversation."

On the walls of his office he had a couple of pictures of Yarmouth sailing ships. On the floor there was a large green carpet. As the years went by it became so faded that the staff wanted to replace it. Killam said it would be extravagance. But it got so worn under the desk that subordinates finally sneaked in a patch. It was the same way in his home. It, too, had an old rug that developed holes that caused people to catch their heals. Killam didn't want it taken out. He said, "All my luck's in it."

In his letter to Sir Robert Borden in 1917 he had said "thoughtful students" agreed with his views. It was a good description of Killam himself. At times, said colleagues, there was almost a dreamlike quality about him. He could sit in his office for long periods, looking out over the St. Lawrence lowlands to the hills of Vermont, thinking, "dreaming up things," making the odd note. He thought elsewhere too. He thought while playing golf, which is one reason he never played it well. He thought during hockey games; it was said of him that he never saw Canadiens' immortal Howie Morenz score a goal, not because he wasn't there but because his mind was on other things. He said himself that he thought 20 years ahead when he looked at a proposition, and people found it was true. "Don't," he once told a subordinate concerned with day-to-day business, "let my needs confuse you. You have your own responsibilities. I'm looking ahead."

Years before research departments became part of financial houses he was a one-man research department. He had a characteristic common to many big men: the talent and the urge to master great detail. "No man today," said one financial analyst, "would master a fraction of the detail Killam had at his fingertips." He could recall sections from old contracts, word for word. One reason: no new contract got by him without meticulous attention. In seeking information, he wanted facts, not guesses. If he asked for a report, he wanted it concise. He once said that if he envied Lord Beaverbrook for any one thing, it was his ability to say things clearly in few words.

He could get to the core of a contract and read a balance sheet "faster than you could blink an eye." He came to know enough about engineering and construction, said Denis Stairs, eventually head of Montréal Engineering, that experts soon learned never to try to put anything over on him. He tended to work from papers, documents, questions. Major decisions were made with deliberation and without haste. He was known, in fact, as a procrastinator.

He believed in having access to the best legal advice he could hire. He worked closely for years in Montreal with Victor Mitchell, then possibly Canada's outstanding corporation lawyer. Mitchell once told a Royal Securities man that Killam came in some ways to know more corporation law than he did himself.

Killam mastered it by working at it. He never went home from the office without a bag full of documents. Night after night he pored over them in the library of the Sherbrooke Street home he had acquired in 1920. On Sunday mornings, for years, he would call his male secretary and politely ask if he had any plans for the day. It was a ritual, and they worked for hours.

Killam struck many people as a cold man, and certainly he could be. He was once described as "Old Stoneface." One lawyer remembered him driving an ice-hard bargain in a real estate deal, them making a generous, soft one with a friend over the same property. For he could be warm and quite sentimental too, especially if someone he knew fell ill. "Then," said a senior Royal Securities man, "the Killam who could be cold and indifferent would go to great lengths to help them." He'd visit them, send gifts, pay the bills.

In the office he was a gentle, soft-voiced man, "an inherent gentleman." If he wanted someone to do something, he would first ask if he were busy. One secretary of Killam's said he never saw him angry in the 25 years they worked together. To another, female, secretary, he was "a lovely man" but a distant one.

The consensus among a considerable number of those who worked for him was that he was "a good man." At least one admired him to the point of veneration. "Killam had no flaws," he said. "He was just odd." They admired him in particular for having strong, even rigid, principles and for sticking to them. "He cut no corners," said one colleague. "He was many times in a position to manipulate the market. He never would."

A financial writer said he had a reputation for being "tough as hell" but honest. A financial man said he "had ethics, and he abided by them," and that seemed to be a common opinion. Said an eminent engineer: "He had to know everything about a project before he would approve it. He was a terrible man to make a bargain with. But once he said 'go' that was it. You could trust him absolutely. He was fair. He was a great man to work for."

Certainly he was, in various ways, an unusual man, so reticent, as one man put it, "that he made me nervous." He even apparently disliked answering the telephone and told his secretary one of his jobs was to keep the press away from him. He was, his sister Elizabeth said, a product both of his Killam background and of his mother's training. "The Killams," she said, "are not a communicative breed. And our mother taught us that we should respect the privacy of others. My brother did respect the privacy of others, and he expected them to respect his."

To close colleagues he was "Walton." Around the office he was apt to be referred to as "I.W." But one result of his reticence was a widespread public ignorance of much or anything about him. Typically, a Montreal doctor who grew up in the city and later came to know them well said he didn't even know who the Killams were when a patient said she worked for them.

He didn't like fuss. He had no side, no pretensions, didn't drop names. He had, said J.C. MacKeen's wife, a large sense of gratitude. His favorite books were detective stories and he read them voraciously. It was said that a doctor once advised him to cut down on such reading. Killam refused. He didn't, said his sister, "like to be told what to do."

It became a legend about him that he never laughed. Actually, friends said, he could be quite witty and funny in a dry kind of way. He had a dry chuckle and if he was really amused he sort of shook all over. The Toronto *Daily Star* in 1927 reported that Killam once sat "with a party of friends in a humorous mood, and as each succeeding rally brought a shout of laughter a young lady seated next to the financier turned to see him sitting silent and unmoved. Half a dozen wisecracks received their applause, and then as one bright effort put the group in a state of collapse, she remarked gently, 'Mr. Killam, if you don't smile I'm going to scream.' Even then he didn't smile."

Yet when the *Star* succeeded a few days later in getting a rare interview, it said Killam spoke of the published anecdote — with a smile. "That young girl," the reporter wrote, "had him all wrong. There is no more sociable man in existence, but he is unique in a world of limelight seekers. He prefers to be an audience. He is like Carlyle. He can have 'a grand talk' without saying anything."

The habit shook one stockbroker, noted for his own quiet character. He once asked to meet Killam. He had no particular reason, he said, but he'd heard a lot about him and wanted to meet him. When he came in, a Killam underling warned him that he had better have something ready to discuss because Killam wasn't much for small talk. The visitor, suitably prepared, went in. He came out a few minutes later, awed and shaken. "My God," he said, "he *doesn't* say much, does he?" He never came back.

Killam smoked a lot of cigarettes. He liked a martini, liked champagne but was never more than a casual drinker. He was listed in *Who's Who* for years as both a Methodist and a Mason. The indications are that he had little to do either with the church or with the fraternal order. He did have a lot to do with clubs. "They were," said the wife of a colleague, "a big part of his life." He was a member of New York's the Links. In Montreal he belonged to two, the Montreal Club on St. James Street and the Saint James's Club, the oldest of the Montreal business clubs, which for many years occupied an ornate four-storey building on a site where the Place Ville Marie now stands.

He was a member of the Saint James's for 40 years, and he contributed to its rich folklore. Once a young, ambitious member of the club came upon Killam in the washroom. He knew the financier had just returned from a holiday in the south, but he wasn't sure where he'd been. He tried anyway. He said he hoped the weather had been good in Barbados. There was no answer. So he said he hoped Killam had enjoyed himself in Bermuda. There was no answer. He tried once more, then gave up. As he left, Killam said one word: "Nassau."

One lawyer said he would always remember the sight of Killam coming into the club and quietly taking his place at a general table where a dozen or so members might be sitting at lunchtime: "He was so diffident you'd think he was the newest member." A more typical picture had Killam sitting at a corner table, all by himself, thinking.

Yet it was the club life of Montreal which delivered a rebuke which stung him and stung his wife even more, and which may well have influenced their attitudes to the entire city. Journalist-author Alexander Ross in his book *Traders* says Killam, like Beaverbrook, was "never fully accepted by the Montreal Establishment" and he cites as evidence the fact that "he was never invited to join" the Mount Royal Club.

The Mount Royal was close to Killam's residence, and it was *the* business club in town, and the fact is that Killam was "pilled," rejected, in applying for membership. The reason, colleagues said, was that rivals in a business deal ganged up on him. Such things were by no means uncommon a generation or two ago but this one added the slings and arrows of Montreal to those Killam had known in Yarmouth, and it may have had longer-range implications.

9

THE PUBLISHER

WHO WASN'T

The spate of publicity about Killam in 1927 was stimulated by his unheralded move into journalism. In October of that year, in what was once described as "the most surprising newspaper sale in Canadian history," he bought the Toronto *Mail and Empire*, a morning daily. It brought down upon him that limelight which he didn't like, and it led to that rare interview in which he charmed a Toronto *Daily Star* reporter. It also brought accolades for his recovery from Riordon.

Toronto's *Telegram* spoke of his "meteoric career." The *Star* called him "a brilliant young financier," a "great promoter." There was, however, one problem. No newspaper could find or get a picture of the new publisher. C.H. Link found them asking and Killam, as usual, refusing to have one taken. Then someone on the *Star* recalled that a photographer had snapped a picture of him at Toronto's Woodbine race track with his fellow Nova Scotian, Ontario's Lieutenant Governor W.D. Ross. It showed his lean, sombre face, typically, beneath a grey fedora, and the *Star* ran it with a feature on Killam's background.

There was, recalled Ken MacTaggart, a Toronto reporter of that era, "great speculation" as to why he had bought a newspaper at all. The strange thing is that, for once, Killam gave his own interpretation. A few days after the *Star*

70

had predicted he would move to Toronto and become active in journalism, a reporter got its interview with him and had the story denied. It headed its article "No Press Czar of Bay Street in New Proprietor of Mail."

"Does your purchase of the *Mail and Empire*," he was asked, "mean that you have wound up the financial page of your existence, and are now going to try out some ideas you have long held as to public affairs and the proper moulding of public opinion?"

"No," the reporter wrote, "Mr. Killam was not out to reform the world. He was not realizing a long cherished secret ambition to own a newspaper. He was not following in Lord Beaverbrook's footsteps.

" 'I am not retiring from financial work,' said he. 'I shall be engaged as actively as ever with the Royal Securities Company. I did not buy the *Mail* because I have long wanted to own a newspaper. I took advantage of an opportunity to acquire what 1 consider a splendid business investment with great possibilities of improvement. I intend to spend as much time in Toronto as I can spare from other activities. It may be that I shall find the newspaper very fascinating. It may be that in six months I shall tire of active association with it.'

"Mr. Killam in brief did not promise to be a new and striking press czar of Bay Street. His role as he saw it would be a coordinating rather than a dictatorial one. As an executive he has had much experience of directing rather than dominating other men's abilities and unobtrusively in the background making the wheels go round. It was clear that in his new situation he was going to feel his way."

The reporter was impressed by the man he met. He sketched his character, his many enterprises, his faith in Canada, and added that he "is a silent man who keeps his reactions to life well locked in a mental safety deposit box . . . But that is not from niggardliness or unwillingness to contribute to the common store of knowledge. It is simply that he has been too busy to pause to tabulate these personal reactions . . . That he is on the whole a silent man does not mean that he is not easy to meet. On the contrary, an interviewer could not meet anyone more affable or amiable or more averse to vitally personal unfolding. . . He has none of the intellectual arrogance of many rich men who, being successful in one thing, are willing to be authorities on everything. There is good warrant for saying that every man thinks he can run a newspaper. But this rich man who now owns a newspaper does not talk that way . . .

"Such modesty in a man of wealth and power was very engaging. It also was a mark of great sagacity. He gave the impression that if he sat back and listened it was not from impassivity; it was from the wisdom of much experience of new situations.

"It would be wrong to form the impression that Mr. Killam is one of those strong silent men with a poker face. On the contrary, his face is very youthful and bland. He has not the square resolute chin of the typical American magazine executive. His manner is not aggressive but gentle. There is no American hustle in his way of walking. He does not swing his arms. He strolls. And seeing him strolling leisurely with the yellow cane that is his constant companion you would take him for a violinist rather than a financier. Despite years of keeping close to the financial grindstone, there is a romantic look about him. He is tall and slender with abundant coal black hair lightly tinged with gray. He would not look out of place strolling about an art gallery."

Killam himself added to that picture a few weeks later in an equally rare public address. He described himself as "a humble apprentice of the press."

Whatever his role, whatever his motives, his politics also worked into the mesh of speculation at the time. The *Mail and Empire* was a Conservative newspaper. The *Star* identified its new owner as "a man of strong political convictions," a Conservative and a protectionist. The *Mail and Empire* itself said that "in politics he is a Conservative." In an interview in London in which he described Killam as "the most brilliant man in early middle age that I know in Canada," Beaverbrook didn't say what he thought Killam's political leanings were but he did utter the intriguing statement that "he had great political ambitions when I found him in a bank clerk's cage in Halifax . . . He has never lost this interest."

If Killam had had political ambitions, the indications were, despite Beaverbrook, that he had put them aside. There

72

had been talk in 1926 of him being asked to run as a federal Conservative candidate in the Yarmouth area. Nothing came of it. His sister once said he could have gone to Ottawa as finance minister, and this report circulated in financial circles as well. Nothing came of that either. The fact was, colleagues say, that he rarely commented on political matters. Colleagues doubt that he ever made a financial contribution to election campaign funds. "You had to guess what he was," said his company secretary.

Certainly *Mail and Empire* editorials did nothing to alter whatever public image Killam had as a Conservative. In announcing his ownership, the paper said it would "maintain the traditions of the newspaper and advocate and support the same principles." Editorially, it remained conventionally and ardently Tory. As for news, Wilf Goodman, a veteran of 50 years of journalism on five papers, said he "never worked on a newspaper where the editorial department had more of a free hand."

Only a few months after he made the purchase, Killam had an exchange of correspondence with Sir Robert Borden, the former Prime Minister, which indicated both Borden's assumption of the Conservative character of the paper, and presumably of its owner, and Killam's attitude towards his own position. Borden wrote on December 15, 1927, to recommend highly the hiring of an editorial writer who was unhappy in his job with another Tory paper. Quite apart from being an excellent writer, said Borden, the man was "a very loyal and devoted supporter" whom he had known "very intimately." Killam replied that he had discussed the matter with John F. Scott, his own managing director, "and I gathered that he is not prepared to take on Mr. ----- at the present time." Then he added that he felt the paper's own leaders "should work out the development of their own organization as far as possible without too much interference from me. We are all very anxious to improve the *Mail* and make it more effective, and I am hopeful that there will be a steady improvement in its efficiency as a newspaper and in its circulation and standing."

It was an accurate indication of Killam's attitude and of his operational methods. He did take the post of president of the Mail Printing Company, and he made it clear that he had no fellow owners. He had asked Saint John, N.B., publisher Howard Robinson to recommend someone he could rely on to run the paper and Robinson suggested Scott, a Saint John native who had worked himself up through the ranks of the Tory Montreal *Gazette* to become managing editor. They had never met, Scott's son said years later, but when they did Scott agreed to go to Toronto as managing director. Killam said at the outset that Scott would be "in complete charge" and that he considered himself "very fortunate" to get him. Newsmen agreed in later years that he got a good man, a small, shy, taciturn man with a dry sense of humor.

Scott was considered "Killam's man" by staffers, and they understood that the two kept in close touch about the financial wellbeing of the paper, one of four dailies in Toronto, and always, it was said, a profitable enterprise. Otherwise Killam was an absentee publisher. On the rare occasions when he did come to the four-storey, red-brick building at the northwest corner of King and Bay streets, he was convoyed around by Scott and would stop to chat briefly and quietly with newsmen. But in general, said journalist Carl Reinke, "he was a ghost as far as the editorial staff was concerned, a gray eminence. We never thought of him."

It was agreed by a number of people that the *Mail and Empire* was a good and aggressive paper in the Killam era, and one major reason stemmed from one of the endless chapters in the often-turbulent history of Toronto newspapers. Shortly after Killam took over, the able Vernon Knowles got into a fight with the *Star's* tough managing editor Harry Hindmarsh and shifted to the *Mail* bringing MacTaggart and two other reporters with him at much better salaries than they'd been making. He became managing editor, hired other good men, insisted on news-page independence, and won.

In the opinion of Ralph Hyman, on the staff for eight years, Knowles was "one of the best newspaper journalists ever produced in this country" and he transformed the *Mail* "from a third-rate Tory sheet to one helluva paper." Said MacTaggart; "It acquired the reputation in Toronto of fearing no man newswise." Said Carl Reinke: "Tory though it was editorially, it carried much more labour news than its rivals, and it was

74

trusted by union men." Never, said Wilf Goodman, "was there a staff so devoted to their paper. They'd stay around in the mornings to check the *Globe*, to see how we'd fared in the search for news." As for Knowles himself, never one to lavish praise, he once said the *Mail and Empire* had the best news staff in Canada.

If Killam noticed, he gave little or no sign that the reporters could see. He did get the paper at his Montreal home, and read it, but the possibility he once held out to the *Star* of becoming fascinated with it never developed.

Nor did the editorial staff mind. As Goodman put it, "Killam may have been a tough man in the financial world. I wouldn't know. But he was good for the *Mail and Empire*." It was a statement at least partly based on personal contact over a delicate matter. Goodman was in charge on the desk one evening when a group of lawyers came in to threaten a libel suit if the paper published one more in a series of articles about a politically-volatile subject. All his superiors were away and, in desperation, he decided he'd have to call Killam.

"I got him at his home," Goodman recalled, "and I told him what was happening. It must have taken me 20 minutes, and he never asked a question till I was through. Then he asked just one. He said, 'Goodman, if you had to do it all over again would you print those stories?' I said, 'Yes, I would,' and he said, 'Then go ahead and run what you have. I'll consult my lawyer in the morning.' " Goodman splashed it on the front page. The lawsuit never materialized.

At the very outset of Killam's days as a publisher, at least one newspaper questioned his acquisition of a paper. An editorial in Montreal's *Le Devoir* expressed grave doubts about him owning the *Mail and Empire*, and saw the possibility of Killam's private interests interfering with his role as head of an organ of public opinion. There was "peril" in the increasing movement of "big business men into journalism. The newspaper becomes merely an instrument. It speaks no longer for the public but solely for a coterie, for private interests . . . The great danger of the press of tomorrow is that it becomes the mere lackey of money."

It wasn't long before that type of question was being asked over a specific issue. Only weeks before Killam bought the paper Royal Securities put out a circular about the possible construction of a St. Lawrence Seaway. It bore no signature but it was a project in which, colleagues say, Killam took a great interest. As such, it is a revealing document, a blend of strong Canadian nationalism and that wariness of the United States that so often gets entangled with it.

The circular was issued in September 1927, just as Conservatives were about to rally for the national convention which picked R.B. Bennett as leader. Circulated widely to convention delegates and many others, widely quoted, the 16-page document was a response to an earlier development: in April, on the basis of a recent engineering study undertaken jointly by Canada and the U.S., Washington had proposed to Ottawa that the two countries launch a speedy development of the St. Lawrence waterway to a depth of 25 feet and build large-scale power developments at various points along it.

The Killam circular was cogent and hard-hitting in its comments. It said the U.S. had "extorted (the word is not too strong)" the right to free navigation through the St. Lawrence in 1871 but what is now proposed "will involve a great addition to the present very limited rights of the United States in and over the St. Lawrence." Canada's right to do what she wished with that portion of the river within her own territory "would be radically impaired the instant the United States became a participant in the cost of deepening and improving the waterway." She would "be the owner of at least a half interest, and probably much more, in this undertaking . . . The examples of the Panama Canal and of the Nicaraguan Canal agreement do not suggest that the Republic will be content to leave that vast investment under the unfettered and unrestricted sovereignty of Canada.

"No adequate price for the surrender of this sovereignty has been offered. It is doubtful if any adequate price could ever be offered. If the United States really needs the waterway, it will eventually cooperate with Canada in the construction of it without demanding any sacrifice of sovereignty. In the meantime, Canada's need of it is not so urgent but that she can afford to wait." The U.S., with its far larger population, would benefit far more than Canada from any waterway. Traffic would for decades be "overwhelmingly American" and it would be difficult to keep the U.S. from regarding it as an American project. It would eliminate the need for most ships to stop at Canadian ports and it would expose Canada to reliance upon a treaty Washington might not be able to enforce if it conflicted with the interests of individual states.

It would be better for Canada to develop her own 68-mile section of the river "in her own good time and upon her own credit." The only part in which the U.S. had to be involved was the 115-mile stretch along the international boundary and that could be handled as a separate thing. This would eliminate all danger of Canada "having a 'Canal Zone' run through her territory and administered by an authority which she herself cannot control."

The circular foresaw the development throwing on the Canadian market a vast amount of power for which Canada had no early use. "A demand would then be made by the United States for the 'temporary' use of the Canadian surplus. The only alternative to acceding would be to allow the surplus to lie idle. Refusal would be practically impossible." And the most compelling fact of all was that "power once exported, even under a limited-term agreement, never returns to the country which exported it . . . To cut it off becomes a moral responsibility . . . There is only one safe way to retain Canadian power for Canadian consumption, and that is, not to develop it until Canada is ready to consume it."

There was still available in the Lower St. Lawrence Basin, and especially on the Ottawa River, "a number of excellent water powers" which "could easily be developed in instalments much more suitable to the annual new requirements of a market of this size." The day would certainly come when Canada would "urgently need" St. Lawrence power and if, because of premature development, it was already being channeled into American industries and cities she would have to turn to more expensive sources.

The circular was issued about the time Killam himself got into Ottawa Valley power development, and at the time when a St. Lawrence development was anything but popular on St. James Street. It was popular, however, in Toronto, and the circular helped stimulate a frontpage editorial attack on Killam and others in the Toronto *Globe* of November 15.

77

Killam took the attack in stride. When the *Star* asked him for a comment that day, all he said was that "it's a fine day for golf." He had just come from Montreal and he intimated that the links there were "just as frigid as the atmosphere in St. James Street when the St. Lawrence scheme happens to be mentioned."

That night he did a most unusual thing. He made a speech. Before the Great Lakes Harbor Association, he said the picture had changed somewhat and he put a different slant on his views. There was, the *Star* quoted him as saying, "no question that the early development of the St. Lawrence waterway is essentially important."

It was, speaking relatively, in some ways a small thing for Canada. "The deepening from here to Montreal is practically a by-product of power development... Apparently public opinion has crystallized on one thing — that power will not be exported from Canada." The U.S., in turn, had now indicated that it was interested only in navigation. Killam thought the question of provincial rights in power should quickly be settled by the courts and Privy Council. "All the power is going into the provinces anyway so it really doesn't matter much what they decide." But the revenue from power "will break the backbone of the cost of the project."

The *Star's* reporter saw his words as "reserved" support for through canalization of the St. lawrence, and his stand as "unconditional even though his announcement was not couched in very strong terms." It was, he wrote, an "entirely unexpected" development. Killam's *Mail and Empire* also reported that he had "endorsed" the project. " 'There are,' he said, 'two million horsepower available from the international section of the St. Lawrence and, of this amount, one million would go to Ontario and one million to the United States. I don't suggest that an immediate market can be found for all of it but if half of it is put into use it would break the back of the cost of this part of the project. . .'

"In Mr. Killam's opinion Canada would have to develop the all-Canadian section ... He urged Ontario Hydro to get behind the development and marketing of its part. If half the three million horsepower in the Quebec section could be marketed, the deep waterway would follow almost as a by-product of the power development."

The *Mail and Empire* had been speaking out editorially on the subject and on November 19 the *Star* undertook to analyze "Mr. Killam's Three Voices" — one in his speech, one in the Royal Securities circular and one in his newspaper. It concluded that "the deduction appears to be warranted that all three believe (a) that the construction of a waterway would be advantageous to Canada, (b) that Canada should construct and control the all-Canadian portion . . . and receive payment from the United States for the use of it and for the use of the New Welland canal, and (c) that the two countries should confer with a view to joint or simultaneous action in the international section of the river, each preserving the sovereignty of its own territory. The proponents of the waterway do not find fault with these propositions and would be pleased to have negotiations begin upon that basis."

A few days later the *Star* published in its news columns under a two-column heading a letter from one T.R. Kirkwood who took a more jaundiced view of Killam's intentions. He saw the speech not as an about-face but as part of a fight by "the super-power interests of Montreal" to block the development and as an effort "to quieten the storm of protest" aroused by the *Mail and Empire's* attacks on the waterway "as soon as Mr. Killam took possession" of the paper. It was clear that Killam would like the waterway developed only after power was developed — and a market found for all of it." And this would take a long time.

In fact, of course, the project was delayed for years. The arguments of 1927 became a premature skirmish in a sporadic battle that culminated in construction a quarter-century later.

10

INTO THE STORM

Five months after Killam bought the *Mail and Empire* there was an announcement which indicated that at about the time of the purchase he had been immersed in the preludes to yet another project. It may help explain his attitude towards the newspaper because the new project was his own, almost from scratch, and it was one in which he always took a deep interest.

In the Nova Scotia Legislature where his grandfather had sat for years, cheers broke out when Conservative Premier Rhodes disclosed on March 7, 1928, that Killam was about to launch "a newsprint development" which would "mean employment of upward of 1,000 men and in addition will afford a convenient and continuous market for pulpwood." He said it would be premature to make any statement about location or any further details. But the next day a reporter caught Killam as he passed through Amherst, N.S., by train enroute to Montreal. He confirmed that he was going to build a paper mill, probably near Liverpool, and said it should cost between $12,000,000 and $15,000,000. The negotiations, he said, had been going on for several months.

The *Mail and Empire* purchase had come out of the blue. Killam's Mersey Paper Co. Ltd. emerged after long controversy rooted in that issue that had stirred Ontario and Quebec in earlier years: the export of pulpwood to the United

States. The struggle was waged on the hustings and in the Legislature, and it may have helped stir Killam's interest. Royal Securities people said one of its executives proposed joining the chorus against pulp export, but that Killam demurred. He wanted to know how much exports meant to Nova Scotia farmers, and he wondered where they'd sell their wood if that market was cut off. The idea was dropped.

Meanwhile from another quarter came a different proposal. J. MacGregor Stewart and J.D. MacKeen, that able legal-business duo who were Killam's colleagues in Halifax, argued that there was another way to absorb Nova Scotian pulp. They argued for what became Mersey, argued that it would not only make money but be a great boon to the province.

In his painstaking way, Killam began to probe the possibilities, visited Halifax frequently, studied every angle, was influenced by a key factor, that the N.S. Power Commission now had the legal tool that could make power sites available. It could expropriate them, and would.

Dr. John S. Bates, a native Nova Scotian and long a noted chemical engineer in the pulp and paper industry, knew Premier Rhodes in high school days in Amherst, and he long had his own story about an episode that may have played a decisive role. He said Rhodes promised Killam cheap power and then questioned him about his ability to finance a mill. "This," said Bates, "struck at Killam's pride as a Nova Scotia-born financier and probably explains his immediate move to go ahead with his own money, without public financing."

Whatever won him over, Killam is said to have gone before a meeting of key men and announced his intentions. "I have looked into all the angles," he is quoted as saying, "I am a bit of a gambler but I only bet on sure things. This is a sure thing. I am ready to back the construction of the mill."

It was far more important news for Nova Scotia than the purchase of a newspaper had been for Toronto. The province had limped along the fringes of '20s prosperity, had turned to Ottawa with cries of Maritime Rights and against unfair freight rates. And nowhere was its relative stagnation more pressing than on the South Shore where Mersey would arise. Liverpool novelist-historian Thomas Raddall knew from personal experience, and he put it into words.

When Raddall came to the area in 1923 those days were long gone when it recklessly exploited its big stands of white pine for ships and lumber, when "nobody cared about the future" and the inevitable eventually happened. He found its economy a gaunt remnant of those halcyon days. When he went to work in the office of the MacLeod Pulp Company at Milton, the basic wage for a 12-hour day in the mills was $2. "No paid holidays, no pension scheme, no insurance plan. If you got sick you were out of luck. The only storage dam on the river was a low wooden thing. Except in very wet summers and falls the mills were shut down from June to November for lack of water, with most .of the hands laid off."

Two small mills above Milton were the biggest single industry in the county and they only employed about 150 men. The price for pulp was $7 a cord. In Liverpool there was a fish plant, a machine-shop, a small bucket factory, a smaller box factory, in Brooklyn a small sawmill. The young, progressive manager of MacLeod Pulp tried to persuade the owners of the Milton mills to modernize. "Unfortunately the owners were primarily timber speculators, mostly American, living far away. As long as the old mills earned enough money to pay the taxes on the timberlands they were satisfied with the crumbling buildings and the obsolete machinery." For years, especially after 1918, "a stream of young men and women had poured out of the county . . . Few ever came back . . . In Queens County, by 1929, there was hardly a family left intact. In many cases whole families had gone."

Small wonder, then, that Killam's decision was big news. It involved, unlike Riordon, a newsprint 'not a pulp venture, and it was not much more than 100 miles from the area where Killam had grown up. There were numerous men who felt that was a key consideration, that amid all his secretive, hard and practical thoughts Killam nursed a deep sentimental attachment to the land of his birth, had great faith in its people. He regretted that so many of them had to leave to make a livelihood.

So he went ahead with Mersey and, Royal Securities men say, he stuck his neck far out. "He risked everything he had." None of the speakers at the official opening of the mill breathed a word about the collapse of the New York stock market, wrote Raddall, "but to those in the know it was plain that Izaak Walton Killam had got a very big fish on a very thin line at the mouth of the Mersey."

"Canada," Beaverbrook's London *Daily Express* had said in 1928, the year before Mersey opened for business, "is perhaps the most enviable country in the world. It is being borne along on a tide of natural . . . and enduring prosperity." On that meretricious tide of the '20s, Izaak Walton Killam rode through the most constructive period of his life. By 1929 he was 44 and he had put together virtually all of that varied, far-flung realm on which he would stake his fortunes for the rest of his days. It employed thousands, extended from the Atlantic to the Pacific, into Newfoundland, Nova Scotia, New Brunswick, Prince Edward Island, Quebec, Ontario, Alberta and other parts of the prairies, British Columbia. It extended into some half dozen countries and colonies in the Caribbean and Latin America. In 1927 alone, among other things, he had acquired a major newspaper, started his power company in the Ottawa Valley, acquired one in Puerto Rico, laid the groundwork for Mersey, nursed B.C. Pulp and Paper and International Power through their infancies, engaged in battle over a St. Lawrence Seaway. He had gone heavily into his native Maritimes themselves. In Nova Scotia alone, said a newspaper in 1929, "his business connections include substantial holdings in such important industries as the Nova Scotia Light and Power Company, Moirs Limited (chocolates), Acadia Sugar Refining Company, the Avon River Power Company, and now the Mersey Paper Company." He had done things which would lead to a *Financial Post* writer's statement of many years later that he "probably did more than Sir Adam Beck (of Ontario Hydro) to electrify the boondocks." He was accepted as one of the big men of Canadian finance, even though few Canadians would have known him if they'd met him on the street.

"He is," reported a writer at the time of Mersey's opening, "a man who has known the varying vicissitudes of fortune, has taken his defeats and enjoyed his triumphs." It had been largely triumphs since Riordon, triumphs borne along on what the *Express* and many others felt to be "a tide of natural

. . . and enduring prosperity." But there was a bleak twist in the turn of phrase. For tides go out, and this one did. It had started out even as Mersey opened for business amid rounds of applause, even as the '20s died away, and even as Killam got used to working with a new right-hand man.

It was said of him not only that he had a talent for picking good men and that he trusted them but that they also stayed with him. But in 1928 his partner, vice president and general manager Ward Chipman Pitfield, had walked out of Royal Securities and established his own investment firm, W.C. Pitfield & Co. No explanation of the split was ever made public, but The Street embodied its suspicions in gossip that it was a bitter one. Indeed, the gossip would grow into reports that they never spoke to one another again, a stark contrast to that day only six years earlier when Pitfield had been groomsman at Killam's wedding.

Now he had left the company, and he was a real loss. He had come from Saint John, N.B., had, like Killam, been "discovered" by Beaverbrook. He had served at the front in the war. He was dynamic, gregarious, and insiders said he and Killam had made a "damned good team . . . Killam was the brain, a sort of dreamer. He came up with the ammunition. Pitfield fired it."

To replace him Killam brought in another outlander, this time from the West. Herbert James Symington was a 47-year-old Winnipeg lawyer and such an exceptional one that Killam's success in hiring him — at a reported $50,000 a year — was considered a major coup. Sir Edward Beatty, president of the C.P.R., told Killam it was the smartest thing he'd ever done, and Sir Edward spoke from experience, and perhaps from gratitude: Symington had built himself a brilliant reputation on the prairies in good part from his assaults on freight rates. His departure, wrote journalist-historian James Gray, was considered a great loss to Winnipeg, especially since he'd thrown in his lot with that eastern financial structure the West saw as its traditional enemy.

Killam had come across Symington through dealings with western grain companies. He made him a vice president, and he looked to him for many things, for legal and other advice, for contacts with Ottawa, for taking that leadership in public which Killam hesitated to take himself. He held in great respect, some say even in awe, this man with a pleasant, winning personality, great gifts, who could run a meeting superbly, could get things done.

Symington didn't fill Pitfield's niche directly. That fell to vice president Albert Culver, a dapper, meticulously efficient businessman known as "Snapper" or "Absolute Al." A native of Winnipeg, a decorated war veteran, he was also a gentleman who could play a tune on the piano once he had heard it. For the Killam-Symington-Culver trio, the staff coined its own nickname, The Trinity, and it was this hierarchy that led Royal Securities into the Great Depression.

If Killam was going to take a long-range approach to investment, he had to be prepared to meet "vicissitudes," to be willing to cope with the erratic character of capitalism, to roll with the punches, to take his chances that things would all work out in the end. It required faith, and he had it. In that 1927 spate of publicity, it had been said of him by "a Montreal financial authority" that he was "a born optimist," a man who thought nationally and "sees a great vision of Canada." Unlike his grandfather, he was, said the Toronto *Daily Star*, "a bull on Canada." Nothing had pleased him more in earlier publicity, he told the *Star* reporter in their interview, than a "statement that he is a Canadian rather than a Montreal citizen." Canada, he once told someone, offered unlimited opportunity for those who were willing to work, to reach out to grasp it. He once said, too, with some regret, that he had found that most people didn't want opportunity so much as they wanted security.

He met the supreme test of both his philosophy and his faith amidst the massive insecurities of the first half of the 1930s, those Depression years that shook the western world to its foundations, counted the unemployed in millions, raised deep doubts about the capitalist system, gave strength to totalitarian movements in Europe, brought Roosevelt's New Deal to the United States, doomed Prime Minister R.B. Bennett's Conservative government in Canada, gave impetus to the emergence of the welfare state, devastated whole industries and none more so than the pulp and paper industry in which he was deeply involved.

There are those who suspect, from certain moves he made, that Killam may have sensed that the Depression was coming. When it did come its impact dwarfed that of 1921 but probably partly because of 1921 he weathered it well. He kept his companies going, often with the help of the banks. He had setbacks, seemed at times, as one colleague put it, "to be completely wrapped up in companies gone sour." But he "lived as though nothing had happened" and he emerged from the worst of it with an enlarged reputation for courage, vision and tenacity. He did so because he saw the Depression, in some ways, as a time of opportunity. He told people it would pass, that Canada had the strength to see it through. He turned it to his ultimate advantage, not infrequently by making moves against the advice of more conventional men. "I could have ended up as rich as Killam," one financial man once said, "if I'd had his guts." In the face of the economic terrors of that time, few men did. Few were willing to take the sort of risks he took.

For months he lay low, watching the firms he owned labouring under ever-gathering difficulties. In Mexico, as one example, continuous losses led in 1932 to abandonment of the street railway operations of his company in Monterey; four years later, as currency devaluations and other problems built up deficits, a sharp reduction was made in capital stock. In Canada, Calgary Power had just nicely gotten its Ghost Development project into operation when slumping markets turned that new power from a boon to largely a surplus, and it would remain that way for years, "Everything," said Denis Stairs, "fell apart all over again." With the Ghost's capital costs to meet, with a lot of money owed to the banks for it, Killam "just kept working away." He worked on franchises, on licenses, on discussions with government, on meeting problems as they arose. "He went into everything in the most tremendous detail." Holding a tight leash from Montreal, Killam plowed his own dividends into the firm, ordered and oversaw extreme care in operations, rigid control on capital expenditures. In 1932 Calgary Power's bank loan stood at $1,800,000; it was paid off in 1934 with returns from a bond issue, and the company came through.

Mersey was another example. Thomas Raddall, then its cashier, once wrote, "The paper market collapsed along

86

with everything else. The price of newsprint went down and down, and even at the lowest point you couldn't sell full production. In the spring of '32 the mill was running only four days a week. It was shut down altogether for half of July and half of August."

Killam had obtained several million dollars from a bank on the security of first mortgage bonds, had planned to sell a second mortgage issue and some of the common stock for several million more. "But," said Raddall in his memoirs, "that plan had gone with the wind from Wall Street. During the first few years of the mill's operation we were paying construction bills out of money received from paper sales and letting huge debts accumulate in other directions, notably the bills of the Nova Scotia Power Commission, which ultimately caused a scandal in the Legislature.

"As contractors and other suppliers came to the end of their own financial ropes and threatened writ and seizure, the bank had to put up more money or see its main loan go down the drain. These additional loans were made through the local branch in Liverpool, whose manager acted as a watchdog for the head office in Montreal."

It had been impossible to sell a planned issue of the first mortgage bonds, and Raddall remembered the atmosphere acutely "because one of my jobs was to go over to the Liverpool branch of the bank almost every day to borrow more money, putting up for security one of those grim forms headed 'Loans Under Section 88 of the Bank Act' . . . in which you pledged everything from the paper on the wharf to the last barrel of pork in the lumber camps.

"For quite a long time we had to go on like this, borrowing money to pay off construction bills and to finance our own payments, the shipments of pulpwood from farmers all over the province, and so on. I remember walking to the bank one day in 1930 or 1931 with one of those forms and telling the manager as casually as I could that the company must have, right away, $300,000. The manager was a man of iron calm, but even his jaw dropped for that one."

Many people thought Mersey was finished, or soon would be. "For a long time," said Raddall, "it was a very close thing." In its first 10 years, indeed, Mersey never paid a cent of dividends. In point of fact, however, it came through the '30s better than most of the pulp and paper industry. It ran most of the time. It sold most of its paper. It made every possible use of the various advantages that had been foreseen in the decision to build it: long-term newsprint contracts that were rare or unique in the business, its position on the seaboard and its ownership of ships which together gave it a $5-a-ton price advantage, its low-price, long-term power contract with the provincial government, and the low cost of purchased pulpwood in large areas of Nova Scotia where there were no competitive buyers, a factor which would stir complaints from pulp producers for years. And, under the ebullient Colonel Jones, the company had good management.

Killam had hired Jones away from a firm in Sault Ste. Marie, Ont. Colorful, dynamic, aggressive, resourceful, a man, in Raddall's words, "with a mind fizzing with ideas," a super-salesman, he proved himself brilliantly. Raddall suspected Killam felt he would need publicity to make Mersey prosper, and that Jones could provide it. He did, and a lot of it was local and pivoted on his own personality.

"Produce," he bellowed at his men. "We'll pile the paper in my office if we can't do anything else." Rotund, merry, vain, he became a Liverpool institution, everywhere known as The Colonel. Every Christmas season he would ride through Liverpool with horse and sleigh, dressed as Santa Claus. For the annual Papermakers' Ball out at White Point Lodge, Jones hauled some guests there by tractor, then led the Grand Parade.

Mersey had a hunting-fishing lodge, and he used it to woo newspaper executives, entertained them royally, saw that they got moose — even, it was said, if a guide had to fire at precisely the same instant as a guest to make sure he didn't miss. He turned a fishing schooner into a yacht for entertainment purposes, too. Mersey's ships' names emphasized the Viking past and Jones used Raddall's talents as a writer and staffer Tom Hayhurst's as an artist in producing two books, one on the Viking era in North America, one on Liverpool's privateering days. He gave a lot to Killam who proudly handed them out. Their real purpose — reinforced by maps — was to stress Mersey's seaboard position, nearer than any other Canadian mill to American markets.

Killam joined those who were out selling its products in those days, so the story goes, even though he had never enjoyed being a salesman. Some people recalled tales of him coming back to his New York hotel room after a day of tramping the streets, looking for business, and calling his wife, often in discouraged tones. Mrs. Killam is supposed to have encouraged him by suggesting that so long as any newspaper was being published, there was a prospect.

He needed little or no encouragement for his habitual eye for detail or for his interest in making Mersey succeed. Premier Rhodes had once said at a happier moment that, in launching the firm, Killam was "as much moved by a desire to render service for his native province as by what I believe to be a profitable business." Whatever the reason, he did keep a close eye on Mersey throughout the Depression, and Frank Covert, for one, came to realize he knew what he was talking about. As a young lawyer, Covert was there one evening when Killam invited Mersey's top men to dine at White Point Lodge. "I thought," Covert recalled, "we'd have some bridge, a social evening. Instead, we sat around a table and Killam pumped them for hours. One thing after another. He was up on it all." And Tom Raddall liked to tell the story of one Mersey financial man who was called to Montreal to see Killam; it took so much out of him he went into hospital for a week.

"Those were tough times," Raddall wrote. "It took a lot of courage not only to operate a business of this size from month to month but to plan a year and even years ahead. Fortunately the owners had these qualities." Fortunately also, he said, so did others associated with the Killams — the Royal Bank which stuck with them, the customers, the workers and managers.

The Depression years produced the only magazine article ever done on Killam in his lifetime, and it makes fascinating reading now if for no other reason than that it catches some of the sceptical mood of the hour. It was written by Charles Vining, a Toronto newsman turned advertising man, and it had an irreverent, collegiate tang which was no accident. Vining had originally written it for a University of Toronto publication, then revamped it for *Maclean's* in 1933.

It bore the meaningless initials R.T.L. as a byline, and it took up only one page in the magazine, a good part of which was occupied by a caricature of Killam. This is what the article said:

Mr. Killam lives in Montreal and is a perfect example of what once was known as the financial magnate, a species rendered almost extinct by the glacial action of frozen assets.

He has a power company in Calgary, a chocolate concern in Halifax, a newsprint enterprise at Liverpool, Nova Scotia, and a good deal of trouble with all of them.

He also owns a newspaper in Toronto called the *Mail and Empire*, and has hoped some day to own the *Globe* as well.

A great many people have wondered why in the world he bought the *Mail and Empire*, and are even more puzzled as to what a man would do with two newspapers, especially two Toronto newspapers.

Such people fail to appreciate the passion of a financier for a merger, which often consists of putting together two mistakes and thus making a bigger one.

Another of his activities is a training school for young bond salesmen known as The Royal Securities Corporation, which has one classroom in Montreal, another in Toronto, and a hopeful spirit among the students.

After he has made a visit to the Toronto office, all his bright young men feel able to tell the boys what is going to happen to the world for the next week or so ...

Mr. Killam has a sense of humor but rarely uses it.

He lives in a rather ugly house on Sherbrooke Street, next door to Lord Atholstan who owns the Montreal *Star* and, through the generosity of Mr. J.W. McConnell, has demonstrated for several years that it is quite possible to have your cake and eat it, too . . .

He does not sleep very well, and blames this on the traffic along Sherbrooke Street except when he is thinking of selling the house.

He has three telephone numbers at his home — one for himself, one for the servants and one for his garage — and could easily get along without the first of these since he rarely speaks on the telephone unless caught unawares.

He does not speak at all unless he has to.

He would rather go around and call on a man than telephone, and would sooner have nothing to do with him than write a letter.

He makes a charming tea guest because he can be parked in a corner and will stay there for a couple of hours without saying anything, especially since the fall of '29 . . .

He is nearly always tired.

His office in Montreal is on St. James Street, a capitalistic thoroughfare inhabited by some distressing cases of arrested mental development and at present in a state of suspended animation.

He was born in Yarmouth, Nova Scotia, sold papers until he was seventeen, and then got a job in a bank, which at that time was regarded as an upward step.

He got out of the bank three years later when Lord Beaverbrook, a permanent adolescent as modest then as now, undertook to show Canada some new altitudes of high finance and started Royal Securities as one instrument of the demonstration.

He was pleased to acquire the Royal Securities business when Lord Beaverbrook subsequently outgrew this country and went over to help England realize that the age of chivalry is past.

He seldom sees Lord Beaverbrook now except when the latter comes back here on some philanthropic mission, such as saving Price Brothers and Company for the sake of the boys.

He has made several million dollars since he left the bank and several years ago was told that he had the smartest financial brain in Canada — a remark which some investors now would be unkind enough to regard as the perfect example of an empty compliment.

He is nearly fifty, wears blue suits, carries a yellow stick, and has romantic brown eyes and a complexion that makes him look slightly in need of a shave.

He made a strict rule some years ago not to be interviewed or photographed by the press, and has had little difficulty about this during the last couple of years.

He is tall, slim, languid and mournful, and is called Ike because his first name is Izaak. His second name is Walton, but this is entirely without piscatorial significance.

He may occasionally be observed sitting sadly with a cocktail in the St. James Club, a business creche located on Dorchester Street and frequented by a number of gentlemen who have nowhere else to go.

The members of the St. James are of two groups: those who wish they belonged to the Mount Royal Club and those who are glad they don't belong to the Mount Stephen.

He sometimes goes to a hockey game and now and then to the theatre, at both of which he displays all the enthusiastic interest of a blind man in an art gallery.

In spite of the inconvenience which frequently results, he is disposed by nature to be friendly with people.

He is even quite friendly with Lord Beaverbrook, although he has known him ever since they were bank clerks together in Halifax thirty years ago.

The article later appeared in a book called *Bigwigs*, published by Macmillans in 1935 and including a series of similar sketches Vining had done on important Canadians of the day. He said in old age that he could see that they must have seemed "scandalously impertinent" at the time. "It was about the first time that someone had done something about our leading men that had an edge to it." He never heard directly from Killam but he says he got word that the financier had taken the comments "fine."

Vining moved into Killam's own sphere just one year after the *Maclean's* article appeared. He became president of the Newsprint Export Manufacturing Association, moved to

Montreal, and became a close friend of Royal Securities' H.J. Symington. He never knew Killam more than slightly, but said long after that he liked him. But Vining never came to consider him "a newsprint figure," an active member of the association Vining led. Killam didn't work that way.

Caricature of Mr. Killam (1933) by Gitano — Courtesy of *Maclean's* magazine.

11

CORPORATE TRENCH

WARFARE

As the Depression ached on and on, someone once asked Killam if he was going south that winter. He said he didn't feel he should; he was so deeply into the banks that he didn't think it would look right.

He borrowed millions of dollars from the banks, mainly the Royal but also others. He was known as "a Royal man," could raise large sums from it simply with a phone call. At times he'd stroll the short distance to its headquarters to talk with Morris Wilson, the native of Lunenburg, N.S., who would become president in 1942. Killam liked and admired Wilson; in time he would establish a university scholarship in his name.

Graham Towers was a rising young Royal executive in those days, and he got to know Killam well and admire him greatly. He admired him for his long-range attitude, for such things as his determination to keep Mersey Paper going even when first mortgage bonds proved almost impossible to sell and a second issue was stalled. "Killam got millions of dollars in debt to the Royal, yes," Towers said in later life, "but it never lost a cent by him. In fact, he never really got too far out on a limb."

It was, indeed, by no means unusual for companies to be far in the red to the banks. "We carried them for millions," recalled a senior banker. "What else could we do? What use would it have been to foreclose so long as they were being run as well as they could be? You had to tough it out. But to tell the truth we were technically broke too. The government saved us with an order-in-council that wasn't made public for a long time. It allowed us to value the bonds we held as security at face value, not the market value to which they had dropped."

Under such circumstances, the web of Killam stories thickened. That he was so far into debt, one subordinate said, he'd never get out, and another said "Don't kid yourself." That management of an insurance firm wanted, even at disaster prices, to get rid of some bonds Killam had sold, and he tried to talk them out of it. They would come back, he said, but when the company wouldn't listen he put a mortgage on his house and did as he was asked.

So the stories went. That Mrs. Killam joked that they'd even mortgaged her furs. That Killam saved several western grain companies by signing their notes. That a bank demanded the money Killam owed and that he stormed in and rasped that "If you had any faith in this country you wouldn't be doing things like this. You'd be mortgaging everything you have and investing in Canada." Then stomped out, borrowed elsewhere, repaid the loan, and never dealt with that bank again. A prominent stockbroker said he'd never heard that story, but it squared with what he knew: "Killam was in debt to us too, and he urged us to see him through because he knew better days were coming."

For months and years they didn't come, and Bruce Hoyland, then Royal Securities treasurer, remembered one day when he had to tell Killam he didn't have enough money to pay the bills and the staff. Killam dug out a cheque folded and folded again, one good for millions. He'd borrowed from the bank and put up one of his properties as collateral. He endorsed the cheque, told Hoyland to take what he needed and bring the rest back in a series of cheques for sums of $50,000 and $100,000.

He may have wanted the money to buy bonds. He'd started to buy pulp and paper company bonds about 1932, and he kept on doing it even though, in the words of one colleague, "he scared the hell out of a lot of us." He scared them because

95

the pulp and paper business was a shambles, much of it in receivership or doomed soon to be. Its stocks and bonds were a drug on the market, drastically down in value. The Depression had caught it in a state of over-expansion and savage price-cutting only made things worse. "Everybody was making secret deals," said one newsprint executive. "Within 20 minutes the news would be all over North America, and the new price would become *the* price." An entire industry seemed at times to be one vast Riordon.

Killam's reaction was to borrow and to buy, and to urge clients to buy. He bought the securities of one company after another for a fraction of their face value. He knew the industry, knew the enormous resources many companies had, to him resources ultimately greater than panic, ultimately more certain than depression. So he bought and, so one more story went, one Royal Securities man kept track of what he did, and did likewise. If Killam had faith in the country, he had faith in Killam. He ended up, in time, as a multi-millionaire.

Alan Gordon, years later a president of Royal Securities, was there the day Killam got word about one financial debacle of the sort that would dominate much of his life during the Depression, would pitch him repeatedly into struggles that came as close as anything could to corporate trench warfare. There would be a lot of them before widespread economic collapse stopped sending shock waves through the financial structure. They would be exhausting, costly, complex and often bitter, and they would consume inordinate amounts of time.

The cheerful, outgoing Gordon was there that particular day by sheer chance. He was a young salesman with Royal Securities in Ottawa, and he and two friends had gone to Murray Bay, Que., very early in the '30s, to live it up at the swanky Manoir Richelieu. Then, to his surprise, the Killams showed up, in their chauffered Rolls Royce, and he met them for the first time. Normally, he said long after, Killam wouldn't have gone there because he didn't like that sort of place, but his wife had lost her sister under tragic circumstances and he wanted to help her get over it.

So here was a young salesman not only meeting the big, mysterious boss but finding he liked him, liked his wife, finding himself dining with them, dancing with Mrs. Killam, playing crap with Killam. And golf.

"We were playing golf one day," Gordon would recall, "when we came to a spot with a magnificent view out over the St. Lawrence. There was a bench there, and on the bench sat one of the leading lawyers of Montreal. He called Killam over, and when he came back he had lost all interest in the game. What the lawyer had told him was that Price Brothers was going into receivership. It didn't take Killam long to head back to Montreal."

His purchase of bonds in one pulp and paper company after another, Price Brothers among them, had put him in a position to have a say in what happened to them, for as long as they failed to generate enough profits to pay interest the bondholders were in the key position. They held, in effect, a mortgage on the property. And what the Dirty Thirties did was precipitate, force Price Brothers and other companies to go through the wringer, to be reconstructed on a new basis because the old basis had collapsed.

Indeed, there was a saying on The Street that there was more money to be made in reorganizing a company than in organizing one: the plant was already there, the staff, the know-how, the structure to work on. The trouble in the '30s was money, and amid its money troubles the pulp and paper industry passed into the second of three phases it would know in Killam's lifetime. It had been to a large extent an industry run by people such as the Riordons who founded firms, often on the basis of an earlier sawmill business. Depression ousted many of them and ushered in the era of the financier, the moneymen equipped to deal with money problems. The time would come for the era of the professional manager, but that had to await the turn of prosperity.

How many troubled paper companies Killam became involved with it is impossible now to say. There were apparently more but in two cases at least he did engage over a period of years in battles for the control of corporate giants, and the first of these was Price Brothers, "one of the great properties in the East."

When it went bankrupt and into receivership Royal Securities held enough of its bonds to provide a key voice as to

97

its destiny. Moreover, Killam had recommended them to others, and one of the cardinal rules of the investment business is that you try to see that a client's money remains secure. He also knew that Price Brothers possessed enormous resources and that it had become a victim of expansion and depression, caught by hard times when it had spent a lot of money on a multi-storied headquarters in Quebec City and on other investments.

The fight for control smoldered for years. As Charles Vining indicated in his 1933 article, it involved Lord Beaverbrook who still held a large block of shares acquired in the 1910 underwriting. It involved Beaverbrook's younger brother, Alan Aitken, who for a time took over the running of the Price firm. It involved other large interests. Scant press notices over a period of years told of Alan Aitken's appointment, of reports that Bowaters, the big British paper company, was moving in, that the question of control remained in the air, that two groups had been formed, that a whole series of re-organizations had taken place. But in the long run it appears to have shaken down to a struggle between Killam interests and the then American-controlled Aluminum Company of Canada.

Alcan was said to have become involved because it wanted to protect its interests under an arrangement which made it and Price Brothers joint owners of a power company on Quebec's Saguenay River, a company to which Price Brothers came to owe a lot of money. It was not interested, one Alcan official said years later, in taking Price Brothers over. But Royal Securities people came to believe Alcan was interested in just that, and Killam was said to have become deeply involved at least partly because he didn't want the firm to pass to American control as Riordon had.

Whatever his motives, he ended up winning. He raised enough money to pay off the bond interest and he got control of a crucial block of shares the Price family had turned over to a bank to back its loans. When the loans remained unpaid the bank put them up for sale. Killam put in the highest bid, and got them. It still was not enough to ensure him control, the sort of 70% control he liked to have. But he did the next best thing. He formed an alliance with two British companies which also held large blocks of shares. That did it.

In 1936 Killam's men took over. H.J. Symington became chairman of the board and Hugh Jones became operating head of both Price Brothers and Mersey. The fight was over. The final phases happened quietly but when the news got out, said Royal Securities' C.H. Link, it was "a sensation" in financial circles. It had been taken for granted on The Street, he said, "that alien control was inevitable."

Even as the Price Brothers' controversy unfolded Killam found himself caught up in another in a quite different field. It involved Famous Players Canadian Corporation Limited, the dominant firm in the Canadian movie business, and it was a sequel to an episode in 1929.

Killam's Royal Securities had been associated with Famous Players since 1920 when it put on the market an issue of preferred shares to allow the company to expand across Canada. It had started that year as a merger of a small number of Canadian theatres put together by Nathan Louis Nathanson, a one-time Minneapolis newsboy who had come to Toronto in 1907, and Famous Players-Lasky Corporation, a Broadway enterprise known as "the largest producers of motion pictures in the world." The new firm got a 20-year franchise to screen the U.S. corporation's films in Canada and the pledge of help in "expert and technical management."

Its president was Hungarian-born Adolph Zukor of New York, "the greatest movie magnate of all time," and head of Famous Players-Lasky. Nathanson was managing director, and Killam became a director.

Nathanson proceeded to build Famous Players Canadian from there. As one *Maclean's* article put it: "Juggling lands, leases, options, stock agreements, booking agreements, contracts and affiliations in a fashion that appealed to bystanders as fantastic, he stepped to one-man leadership of a whole industry," became known as the "Napoleon of the Canadian screen." Then "talkies" emerged in the late '20s to replace silent movies and big interests began to war on an international front for the whopping financial rewards they promised. In the words of one journalist, "sound was the equivalent of gold."

Amidst this, a move was made ostensibly to bring the firm under Canadian control. Zukor agreed to sell on the

Canadian market the controlling shares held by Famous Player-Lasky, now known as Paramount Famous Lasky Corporation and soon to become Paramount Publix Corporation. But there was a crucial reservation: to protect its Canadian market the shares were to be placed in trust and sold as trust certificates, and three voting trustees, Zukor, Killam and Nathanson, would have the final say in company operations.

Royal Securities and another investment firm put the so-called voting trust certificates on the market at $51 apiece while Nathanson proclaimed that the company now was a "100% Canadian owned and operated company." In fact two men, by banding together, could make the company's ultimate decisions and the continuing presence of Zukor as president indicated that he remained the pivotal figure; he controlled the company's pipeline to prosperity, the films it screened.

It wasn't long before the triumvirate was put to a test precipitated by Nathanson. His goal, he said later, was to "convert Famous Players Canadian into part of a tremendously bigger thing . . . To produce (British) Empire pictures in a big way," to make in Canada 50 pictures a year so good they would sell anywhere, and to declare independence from American control by creating a company "big enough to tell Adolph Zukor that Canada . . . was no longer a spoke in his wheel."

Nathanson set off for London in the summer of 1929 with a grandiose plan: to buy or to merge with Gaumont British Pictures Corporation to produce a company to do battle with American interests. But there he found that America's Fox Film Corporation had bought 27% of Gaumont's common stock — and Fox was fast rising as the most serious challenger to Zukor's control of American filmdom. "I was too late," Nathanson later said. But he wasn't too late to come up "with the next best thing," which was, he said, to talk Gaumont into offering $75 apiece for Famous Players Canadian voting trust certificates recently put on the market for $51, in effect to take the firm over.

Controversy quickly developed. Nathanson repeatedly insisted that Fox had no real control over Gaumont because the British had taken steps to see that its shares did not entitle it to vote on company decisions. But Killam and Zukor banded together to block the offer from being placed before Famous Players Canadian shareholders. In the later words of a director, "upon investigation, the directors were satisfied that the Gaumont Company was contròlled by American interests, therefore the board decided against proceeding further with such negotiations."

A Toronto *Telegram* reporter tried to get Killam himself to comment — and as a result gave a succinct picture of a typical Killam stance in such a situation. "Mr. Killam would say little," he reported. He left most of the talking "to a companion who smilingly denied that he was H.J. Symington (Royal Securities vice president). The whole reason for rejection of Nathanson's plan, said the latter, was that the Gaumont Company . . . was an American-controlled concern."

With that rejection, Nathanson resigned as managing director.

Killam's own position at that time was described by a Toronto *Daily Star* writer as that of a man who "has been very necessary to F.P.C. But for him the company, even with Nathanson's ability, would not have been where it now is. He had no personal ambitions in the company. He did not aim to control it. What control there is outside of the company itself in Canada is held by Zukor."

In 1931, before an official inquiry into the movie industry in Canada, Killam finally did talk publicaly about these events. His version was that he'd first thought Nathanson's original proposal of a deal with Gaumont was "in general . . . a good idea" because he understood Gaumont was in British hands. But, later, Nathanson had "admitted quite frankly to me that Fox was the buyer in substance as well as in shadow and that Fox, of course, would not make the offer in the open."

As a sequel to the episodes of 1929, Famous Players Canadian once again passed into the control of Zukor's Paramount Publix Corporation through a controversial 1930 exchange of shares that was battled by a small group of shareholders. The change was precipitated, Killam said, by fears that Nathanson, now head of Regal Films, would combine with Fox to set up a rival chain of theatres across

101

Canada and put the industry in a troubled position akin to that of pulp and paper. There was also a second reason: Zukor didn't want to see a repetition of the 1929 threat of outside control, and this seemed to be the best way to head it off.

At the same time, wrote James A. Cowan in *Maclean's*, Famous Players Canadian's dominant position in Canada was a key to "evident dissatisfaction with conditions as they exist in the land of make-believe and make money." As controversy grew in Parliament and the press, an organization known as Exhibitors Cooperative Association and proclaiming itself to be the voice of "the little fellows" demanded a probe under the Combines Investigation Act. In 1931 the request bore fruit. The Bennett government appointed Peter White as a one-man commission under the act to conduct an inquiry into the movie industry in Canada.

It was at this inquiry that Killam testified. He held that Zukor's Paramount Publix didn't control Famous Players Canadian, that he and Nathanson — still a voting trustee — "could turn out Mr. Zukor tomorrow." He agreed that this was unlikely to happen "as I size up Mr. Zukor. But if I thought he was doing wrong I would do it." He defended the transfer of Famous Players Canadian shares for those of Paramount Publix as "very proper" and said it would give shareholders a wider and stronger base for their investments.

The upshot of the inquiry was White's finding that Paramount Publix was in "virtual control" of Famous Players Canadian "by its ownership of 93.786% of the issued shares" and that this was so regardless of the voting trust agreement. As a result, the federal government launched a legal action in 1932 only to have it dismissed in the courts.

A year later the Depression put Paramount Publix into receivership and new questions were asked both about the exchange which had swapped Famous Players Canadian shares for its own and about the denial in 1929 of an opportunity for shareholders to pronounce upon the alleged willingness of British Gaumont to buy Famous Players Canadian shareholders' stock. Paramount Publix stock, worth $77.25 in 1930, now sold at 97 1/2 cents. On May 7 Famous Players Canadian reported a sharp drop in its own earnings and said operating conditions were "very unfavorable." Then came a startling climax. On May 31 the press carried stories announcing "radical changes" in its board. Most notable of all was the news that N.L. Nathanson had been installed as president, that Adolph Zukor had become chairman.

A spokesman said "several former members of the board were asked to remain but owing to business commitments and obligations were unable to accept." At the meeting which ushered in the changes a shareholder asked whether the three voting trustees remained the same. Said a Toronto *Daily Star* story: "The answer was given in the affirmative." But the difference this time, it was explained by the chairman, "is that Adolph Zukor voted with Mr. Nathanson instead of with I.W. Killam as formerly." It was, said the *Financial Post*, "a brilliant volte face of events for Mr. Nathanson." As for Killam, he expressed his displeasure in his own way. On that same May 31 he resigned as a director.

The exact circumstances of the shift that restored Nathanson were never made public. In the *Financial Post's* opinion, the key was that Paramount Publix wanted him back, that to counter the inroads of the Depression they now felt he "was important" to success.

Typically, Killam offered no public comment on Nathanson's return to power or on his own resignation as a director. He'd won one and lost one in the struggles involving Nathanson. He was, colleagues said, bitter over the defeat.

12

AND MORE OF IT

Only shortly after the successful conclusion of the Price Brothers affair, Killam was in the news again. As suddenly and unexpectedly as he had bought it, he sold the *Mail and Empire* to a striking new duo in Toronto financial circles. One was William H. Wright, an aging Cockney, a veteran of the Boer War who had come to Canada in 1907 with $10 in his pocket. He fought in World War I as a "millionaire private"; he had gone prospecting, struck gold and become wealthy. Now he was wealthier still, and he had formed an alliance with handsome, driving 31-year-old George McCullagh, a one-time London, Ont., newsboy, a former employee of the *Globe* who had turned stock promoter.

In October 1936 they bought the 92-year-old *Globe*, and McCullagh promptly proceeded to dazzle the city with changes. Under pious publisher William Gladstone Jaffray, it had used no racing news, no movie gossip or tobacco advertising, and every Wednesday Jaffray had bestowed upon his readers the blessings of a sermon. Under McCullagh, it started to run tobacco ads, racing tips and track results, to buy in New York all the comic strips and news features it could get. Recalled reporter Ken MacTaggart: "He ran stories outlining his plans — the Biggest and Best of Everything."

Even as the *Mail and Empire* reacted by trying to round up extra comics for itself, gossip spread that McCullagh's next target was a merger of the two morning papers. He let the word get around that he had the money and the intention to make things rough for the *Mail and Empire*, and that he felt there just wasn't room in town for two morning dailies. Then out of the blue, he later told MacTaggart, he got word from Killam that he'd like to come to Toronto to see him. They met the next morning over breakfast at the Royal York Hotel. It had been rumored in the past that Killam might try to buy the *Globe*, but when the dickering was over he was the ex-newsboy who had agreed to sell.

McCullagh later said privately that he *had* stressed that Toronto wasn't big enough for two morning dailies, that Killam would be in a difficult position as an absentee and inactive publisher living in the rival city of Montreal. The negotiations, he added, were "comparatively easy and of the most pleasant nature."

The *Daily Star* saw the purchase as "a dramatic stroke." McCullagh saw it opening the way for the Toronto morning field to "be served by one great metropolitan paper." There was no announcement of the price Wright and he paid but it was reported to be in the vicinity of $2,500,000 for the paper alone. Since they intended to erect a new building, they had no need of Killam's real estate. He peddled that, in turn, for another reported $2,500,000 or so. In total he probably more than doubled what he'd put up in 1927.

The night of the announcement of the sale, the *Mail and Empire* staff staged an all-night wake at a downtown hotel. Many of them were bitter that Killam had sold to what they saw as an inferior rival, especially when the paper had started to do better financially now that the worst of the Depression was over. Most had deep personal doubts about their future. So did the less competent members of the staff of the *Globe*.

Colleagues say Killam felt he had assurances from McCullagh that he would look after the *Mail and Empire* people. McCullagh himself announced that so far as might be "compatible with good business practice and efficiency" as many as possible would be employed with his newly-named *Globe and Mail*.

He did take on a staff "much larger than was necessary," said MacTaggart, but for a considerable number there were no jobs. In the *Globe and Mail* of November 26, ex-*Mail and Empire* columnist J.V. McAree spoke out in behalf of men "of the highest decency" who were "threatened with unemployment, threatened indeed with ruin" because it had been "profitable to abandon them." McCullagh, he said, was paying four weeks' wages to those who had no work but he had no legal responsibility to do so. The legal and moral responsibility rested in Izaak Walton Killam.

Meanwhile, the *Mail and Empire's* last managing editor, Bob Farquharson, had set up shop to do what he could to help. In doing so, he made a trip to Montreal to see Killam and acquaint him with the facts. He later said he was surprised by what he considered the generosity of the response. Killam gave him a cheque for $50,000 and told him to look after the unemployed men as he best saw fit.

On January 6, 1937, the *Globe and Mail* said that because of Killam's act editorial staffers who still had no work would get one week's pay for each year on the paper. Others for whom, for various reasons, further employment was impossible would be pensioned. As things turned out, Farquharson didn't use up quite all of the $50,000 Killam gave him. Years later his wife was surprised to find a Toronto bank account he had forgotten. It was one started with Killam's money. In it there was just over $200 left.

In the last stages of its existence the *Mail and Empire* had been drawn into an issue which locked another Killam enterprise in controversy for months. It waxed in the courts. It brought stormy scenes to the Ontario Legislature. It involved Killam's Ottawa Valley Power Co., and it pivoted around Ontario's swashbuckling Liberal premier Mitchell Hepburn.

In opposition, before his election to office in 1934, Hepburn had been attacking certain power contracts signed by the Conservative Ferguson government in the late 1920s. There were four of them, Ottawa Valley's and three others. Under them, power generated in Quebec was fed into the lines of Ontario Hydro in what Hepburn charged was a "wasteful" way. He promised action in the Legislature when and if he came to power.

He was true to his word. A week after the 1935 session started, Hepburn's Attorney General, Arthur Roebuck, made a three-day assault on three of the four contracts and contended they were costing Ontario millions annually for unused electricity. He assailed them as benefits to "big interests," called them "not only outrageous and inequitable, but illegal and unenforceable." Ontario and Quebec, he maintained, did not have the authority to negotiate them.

On April 1 Hepburn introduced a bill declaring the agreements with the three Quebec companies to be "illegal, void and unenforceable," and including a clause barring them recourse to the courts. "Ontario today," said Hepburn, "is in an impossible position . . . The Province is bound for a period of 40 years to purchase huge quantities of unwanted power from Quebec." Dogged by depression, industry simply couldn't absorb it.

Amid protests from the *Mail and Empire* — it compared the action to Germany's repudiation of the rights of Belgium in 1914 — from the Investment Dealers' Association of Canada, from the press and the Conservative opposition, the bill was debated for days and nights. Then the overwhelming Liberal majority put it through.

It brought, Hepburn said, private threats from Quebec Premier Taschereau to shut off all power export from Quebec to Ontario. To that, he replied that Ontario was "prepared to defend ourselves in an economic war which would do his province more damage than it would ours." In fact, before the new act was proclaimed two of the four companies had come to terms on new contracts at lower prices. But for Ottawa Valley the axe had fallen. In response, Killam went to court to test the validity of both the contract and its cancellation in a case said to involve some $60,000,000 under a 40-year deal calling for Ontario to take 96,000 horsepower.

Then in February 1936 Hepburn charged that Killam's *Mail and Empire* had benefitted economically from the contract held by Ottawa Valley. "The Province," he said, "was the *Mail and Empire's* 'sugar daddy.' " The people of Ontario had in effect paid money to "bolster up" the paper "when it was in difficulties."

The paper responded hotly: "The Ottawa Valley power contract neither helped nor injured the *Mail and Empire*, nor has the cancellation . . . affected this paper in the slightest degree." It had "never required 'bolstering,' nor has it accepted financial assistance from any source . . . The *Mail and Empire* has shown a satisfactory profit every year . . . has always been operated as a separate entity. No attempt has been made to control either its editorial or its news columns."

By June the court's decision was announced. Without reaching the basic question of the validity of either contract or the cancelling legislation, Chief Justice H.E. Rose of Ontario dismissed Ottawa Valley's action with costs. The company promptly appealed, and on November 19, before "a tense, well-filled courtroom anxiously awaiting the verdict," the Appeal Court announced good news for Killam. By a 3-2 decision, it held sections of the 1935 Act to be ultra vires of the Legislature, held that Ottawa Valley had a right to bring against Ontario Hydro an action seeking a declaration that the contract was valid and still in force. It overruled Chief Justice Rose's finding that a clause in the Power Commission Act granted Hydro immunity from suit.

As Ottawa Valley bonds rose sharply in value — they had dropped earlier — Hepburn called the decision a hollow victory for "the Tory party and the power barons of St. James Street" and pledged a fight to the finish. He accused his friend George McCullagh's new *Globe and Mail* of reversing its policies and advocating "the interests of the financial ring whose yoke the government has struck from the power users."

He raised the Killam issue again too. He said "The *Globe's* stand has been in marked contrast to that of the former *Mail and Empire*. The latter paper has been outright in its advocacy of the power interests, but its influence has been nullified by the known fact that it was purchased by Mr. I.W. Killam . . . for the very purpose of putting across the Ottawa Valley Power deal, and further by the public knowledge that this gentleman is still interested in very large figures in power contracts."

In January 1937 Hepburn introduced a sweeping amendment to the Power Commission Act which would render all the property of Ontario Hydro exempt from any and all processes of law which might follow judgment or order of any court of the province. Yet even as it was debated another element was coloring the issue. "Industry's steady return to normal conditions," as one reporter put it, now was raising the spectre of a power *shortage*. Liberal Members of the Legislature had become "extremely jumpy over persistent suggestions" that one was shaping up. Conservatives added to their discomfiture with warnings in the House. Already, it was reported on January 22, there were rumors that negotiations were going on with Ottawa Valley Power Co. "to establish sufficient of a Hydro reserve to take care — beyond all doubt — of any power demand situation which may develop shortly in Ontario."

Less than a month later the story proved true. Said a news story on February 13: "The long-standing dispute between Hydro and the Ottawa Valley Power Company ended yesterday with ratification by the Hepburn government of a revised power agreement." Under it, Hydro bought the output of Ottawa Valley for $12.50 per horsepower, a cut from $15; the company agreed to end its law suit; it also agreed, as it hadn't earlier, to bear any taxes that might be levied against it by Ottawa or Quebec Authorities.

In the end, it was a compromise. The Premier, wrote Neil McKenty in his biography *Mitch Hepburn*, did get better terms, "but it was still humiliating" for him to renew contracts he had cancelled and vowed he would never sign again. As for Killam, he may have been glad to have the struggle over but he was hardly happy about the result.

Years later Montreal Engineering's Denis Stairs said Killam accepted the new contract reluctantly and only because he was running short of cash for Ottawa Valley even as there was a threat that the bondholders might take over. It meant less return on his investment, exposure to the threat of more taxation and, said Stairs, was in fact "a very poor contract."

It had been Stairs, on a picnic, who had first come across what became the site of the Chats Falls project. For some time it had seemed that Killam would go on up the Ottawa River, building more dams as he went. Among its other effects, the 1937 contract put an end to that.

Killam had kept a characteristically low public profile in the power issue, in the Price Brothers issue, in his ownership of the *Mail and Empire*, and his quiet, gradual accumulation of the securities of one company after another. He had lived up to the *Daily Star's* 1927 picture of him as an executive with "much experience of directing rather than dominating other men's abilities and unobtrusively in the background making the wheels go round."

He did it again in two more controversies that moved through the '30s and on into the years of World War II. The first concerned control of the Abitibi Power and Paper Company with its five newsprint mills and other plants stretching from Beaupre, Que., to Pine Falls, Man., but mainly concentrated in Ontario. Founded in 1914, it defaulted in 1932 on an interest payment on $48,000,000 worth of bonds which Royal Securities had helped sell in 1928. It went into receivership, a giant caught in an entire industry's web of collapse, a glittering prize up for potential grabs.

Out of this there developed once more a collision between two groups, people who held Abitibi bonds and people who held common and preferred shares. Both formed committees to fight for them, and Killam's right-hand man, H.J. Symington, emerged as chairman of a group representing those with a majority of the bonds and thus the prior claim. On the other side, Toronto's Harry Gundy, potent head of the Wood Gundy & Co. investment firm, was a crucial figure among the shareholders.

The struggle was fought in the courts, the press, board rooms, behind the scenes and on the floor of the Ontario Legislature. It grew, as one participant put it, until it embraced a period of "dark and stormy years." A number of reorganization plans were worked out. They got nowhere. By 1940 it was still a stalemate and wartime conditions had made Abitibi a richer prize than ever because it was enjoying substantially higher earnings. But by then unpaid bond interest had accrued and compounded to $24,000,000 — half the value of the bonds on which Abitibi had defaulted eight years before.

The struggle dragged on for another three years. Through a court order for sale. Through pressures from Ontario Conservative leader George Drew for the Hepburn government to do something and Drew's appeals to the bondholders not "to freeze out" the shareholders, "having in mind the importance of maintaining public confidence in corporation securities in such critical times as these." Through statements in court that the bondholders committee saw it as "their duty to buy the property at the lowest possible price." Through attempts by both Drew and shareholders to get Symington to change his tactics, only to get a reply quoted as "once a mortgage, always a mortgage. We intend to foreclose." Through a sale that solved nothing: Symington's committee bid $30,000,000, comparable to the value of its majority share of the bonds on which Abitibi had defaulted, only to have the offer thrown out because it was below a bid level set by the courts. Through a 1941 Royal Commission and then legislative action by Hepburn in keeping with its findings: a Moratorium Act designed to stall a second sale. Through two court rulings declaring the Act invalid. Through further Conservative calls for Hepburn to use all possible powers to sway the bondholders committee. Through Hepburn's 1942 action in bringing in bills to stall a sale still further and to grant Abitibi the right to appeal the court decisions on the Moratorium Act to the Privy Council.

Hepburn was no longer the militant, bombastic leader of old but he was still capable of castigation. He said the bills represented about all he could do: "I must confess I have exhausted all my other resources. I don't know whether my honourable friend is acquainted with Montreal financiers but Mr. (Howard) Ferguson, when he was Premier, tried to intervene and he called Mr. Symington a 'cold north wind.' We could use the powers of the Lands and Forests Department, but we have no complete authority." If he did cancel the company's timber licences it would throw thousands out of jobs and stop essential war work. Through the bills, he was doing what he could to "save the company from the wolves of Montreal."

So the case went to London and there the Privy Council found the Moratorium Act constitutional. It set the stage for resolution of the dispute but that didn't come till after Hepburn had resigned in October 1942 and Drew had come to power in August 1943. Drew named a committee to get Abitibi, now operating at full capacity, out of receivership. He said he would bring in legislation if it was impossible to get voluntary agreement for the committee's plans. It worked. With this warning, with its arguments rejected by the

Commonwealth's highest court, with its objectives assailed by both old-line parties, the bondholders committee agreed to negotiate. They had not been acting in any unique way in such fights — bondholders had frozen out shareholders in the Riordon confrontation, as one example — and they had been entirely within the law in everything they did. But the tide had turned against them.

Representatives of the various groups were named to a new body to supervise the company. The bondholders held the decisive positions, but they assumed that once their interest was paid off they would be ousted. It didn't work out that way. The interest was paid off within a few years, but things were going well and the same group went on running them. As the climax to it all the company was taken out of receivership in 1946. Killam got his delayed interest back and so did bond buyers who had bought their securities from Royal Securities.

The second controversy embroiled Killam's power company headquartered in San Juan, Puerto Rico, and operated as one of the subsidiaries of International Power. This too went on for years and came to a solution about the same time as the Abitibi case.

Paul Raymer, an American-born engineer who was with International Power for nearly half a century, was manager in San Juan then, and his recollection is that the trouble started in the '30s when President Roosevelt's pump-priming New Deal measures penetrated what was then an impoverished American colony. "Puerto Rico had a lot of unemployment," Raymer said, "and the New Deal came in pouring out money. The government of the island owned some irrigation companies and they began to build them up. They bought a cement works, and they wanted power. They began to build their own power facilities."

When Killam reacted and began to fight this threat to his Puerto Rico Power Company he found himself with a court battle on his hands. The government seized his company and put up $6,000,000 in recompense. Killam said it wasn't nearly enough, but a Puerto Rico court found against him.

By law, there was a right of appeal to the courts of Massachusetts. Killam exercised it, and won: it was ruled that Puerto Rico Power must be returned to its owners. The government didn't appeal; it simply seized the company all over again. Killam promptly took the case back to the local courts, lost and once again carried an appeal to Boston.

By this time Washington had decided to take its own measures. The Roosevelt administration, said Raymer, sent a high official to Montreal to propose a settlement out of court. Killam had the original $6,000,000 in a bank but he informed the emissary that it was well below what he was prepared to accept. It developed into a battle of willpower, while the court case stood in abeyance and Killam sounded out associates for opinions as to whether he should continue to fight or should sell if he got his price. Raymer's opinion, as manager, was that in the light of what could be done to the company through taxation and other measures he would be wise to sell.

Killam did but he harvested a rich bounty for the battles he had fought and the stubbornness he had shown. "He fought them to a standstill," said a colleague. In the end, said Raymer, he got what he wanted, got at least twice the $6,000,000 and perhaps even more than that, "every cent of it cash on the barrelhead." It was the one time in his years of controlling International Power that one of his subsidiary companies was, in effect, confiscated in the world of banana republics, and company executives found a touch of irony in the fact that it was done under the aegis of the American government.

Killam promptly had another court battle on his hands, over what price should be paid to preferred and common shareholders in settling the affairs of the company. But most of the money went to him anyway as by far the largest of the lot.

It came in handy. To the encroachments of the Depression had been added the ravages of hurricanes. There were power lines to be rebuilt, other things to do especially now that war had come. "That money," said Raymer, "put International Power on its feet. We needed it for growth."

13

THE GLITTERING

PUPIL

When King George VI and Queen Elizabeth came to Montreal on their triumphal Canadian tour of 1939, the Killams responded grandly. They draped every window at the front of their home with Union Jacks, entertained guests at dinner, then went down to Dominion Square to join the thousands who turned out in greeting.

Yet Killam saw, had seen war coming, just as he may have seen the Depression coming. As the tattered '30s neared their end and the international situation deteriorated, he came to fear the worst, and he talked about it in an open way some people hadn't heard him use before. At the time of Munich in 1938, when Britain's appeasing Neville Chamberlain flew home from a meeting with Hitler bearing what he called "peace in our time," Prime Minister Mackenzie King ecstatically approved but Killam doubted. He told a subordinate there would be war, and when war did come he seemed to know a lot about the inherent weaknesses of Britain's defences, and the months of early stalemate, of "phony war," didn't fool him. He feared it was going to be a long and difficult struggle and said "this fool Hitler has declared war on the whole world."

As the long and difficult struggle did develop, he found his own business marking time, the government taking over the bond market, dictating to industry and finance as it never had before, his staff denuded of some of its best men, of Symington, Stairs and others. Killam remained behind, living in a world in which business had to take a back seat. He held on to what he had, and watched the war put strength where Depression had put weakness. He put Royal Securities once again behind War Loan drives. He fretted; a relative who visited him one evening found him concerned about his Mersey ships as the submarine war pressed westward to the very shores of North America. His worries weren't without foundation: two of them were sunk. And he came to one of the low points of his life in 1944 when his sister Elizabeth Rodgers' son Walton was lost in air action with the American forces in the Pacific. Walton Rodgers was his great favorite, some think his choice as the heir to his empire. Childless himself, Killam had sent him to Mersey in the '30s to start learning the ways of business. He took the death very hard.

Like all men's, the profile of Killam's own life had adhered to the pattern of his times. He was born in the era of swashbuckling individual business initiative and the sailing ship; he would die in the era of big government and the atomic bomb. He had gone through the Laurier boom, war, depression, boom, far greater depression, war. Through it all, he had, in a sense, grown a tree with faith that the soil was there, despite everything, to make it prosper — if he gave it time, if he held on and worked hard.

It worked out too. In his 50s the tree began to bear a bounty of fruit. World War II, that artificial agent which banished depression, firmed its roots, nourished its growth. The prosperity that followed added emphasis and momentum to the process. "From 1939 on," said a newsprint executive, "everything went right for Killam."

In Mexico, as one example, the firm in Monterey was enjoying stability after its years of troubles. According to a calculation made in 1975, a company in which Killam's original investment was $3,608,797 had realized in 47 years $8,329,495 in principal amounts, $5,715,958 in interest payments, $1,796,000 in preferred and common stock dividends — and International Power held company stock worth $5,900,000.

The Canadian pulp and paper industry, as another instance, had rallied in the war despite labor and other shortages and, with the return of peace, passed into a decade of sunshine such as it had never known. A 1948 prospectus for an offering of 15,000 preferred shares of Mersey Paper stock gave one indication of the change. It showed that the company's gross profits had quadrupled between 1938 and 1947 and were up notably again in the first six months of 1948, to more than $2,000,000. Six years later, when Mersey celebrated its 25th anniversary, the Halifax *Chronicle-Herald* noted that it was still Nova Scotia's second industry, that it had doubled its output in that time, had produced 2,553,000 tons of newsprint, had benefitted not only from "additions to plant and the installation of the latest types of machinery, but also because of the cooperation and incentive of its employees and the goodwill of its customers, friends and neighbours." No less than 159 of its employees had been with the firm for the entire 25 years, "surely a remarkable commentary on employer-employee relations." And the man who had made it all possible, said the editorial, was I.W. Killam.

Killam's Calgary Power Ltd. gave another indication. It had weathered the prairies' savage Depression and now it too had responded to changing times. By 1946 production was up sixfold since 1925, revenues up tenfold. In 1947, the year Leduc's discovery signalled the beginning of what became Alberta's oil boom, the company's headquarters were moved from St. James Street to Calgary. Its ambitions had to stop short of a successful invasion of Edmonton — the provincial capital sat on a coal bed and had power of its own — but now its transmission lines threaded through large areas and it had become one of the big industries of a province soon to become one of the most prosperous in the land. In 1948 it began a major thrust for farm electrification — and found itself involved in political controversy.

Alberta's leftist C.C.F. (Cooperative Commonwealth Federation) party had long advocated public ownership of power, and had at various times received considerable support for its views from farm organizations and rural electrification associations. As the pressures built up, the Social Credit government decided that year to make private versus public ownership of power companies an election issue and to give the people a chance to declare themselves through a separate plebiscite. The government itself actively advocated private ownership, and the plebiscite confirmed this view.

With that behind it, Calgary Power became the largest investor-owned electric power company in Canada. By 1956 its production would be up threefold again, its revenues up fourfold, and surging growth would go on from there. It had, claimed an executive of the firm, had "consistently good relations with its employees over the years," had never experienced a major strike or serious work stoppage.

Killam was proud of it. In one of his rare expansive moments, he had once said that it would do big things for the West, and the postwar years confirmed his statement.

But it was a changed Killam who faced into those years, and the change went back to the Depression. The corporate struggles, the economic strains, the erosions of the '30s took a great deal out of him. Quite simply, said his sister Elizabeth, they ruined his health. He had a coronary thrombosis in 1946. He had to watch his heart carefully now, and because he had never been much for exercise he had to watch his liver too. He had high blood pressure. He was supposed to be on a diet but tended to ignore it. Moreover, his wife developed cancer and had two operations which left both of them fearful for years of a repetition. She developed arthritis. She had back trouble.

For these reasons, for others, Killam was a different man now, a less assertive man, though he could be unpredictable about it. He had built an empire, tapped enormous resources and produced great wealth, colleagues felt, not primarily out of desire for great personal wealth but for the sheer satisfaction of achievement, the joy of creativity. "He was like a golfer," said one, "he wanted to better his score." No one enterprise alone had made him but now he had enough and he was largely content to hold on and see it grow with a growing, booming country. He began to talk a bit about his wealth, which was something he had never done.

Back in 1937 a newsman had described him as "probably the least known of Canada's wealthy men." By 1948 *Fortune* magazine was reporting he was "said to be the richest man in Canada." In 1951 Lord Beaverbrook told a *Time* correspondent he agreed and estimated Killam's wealth at $75,000,000 — though he later admitted he really wasn't sure. Yet Killam remained a man of mystery, the sort of man Robert Fowler saw when he called on H.J. Symington after becoming head of the Canadian Pulp and Paper Association: "We were sitting there talking when I became aware that someone had slipped quietly into the room. It was Killam. He didn't say a word. He just stood there, looking over the new boy. Then he went out as silently as he'd come in." He had long ago been described as a man with "few familiars" and now he struck various people as a lonely man, a loner paying a loner's price.

The once black hair was white now and, said Alan Gordon, "no one around the office would have thought of calling him anything but Mr. Killam." Now the banks wondered why Royal Securities did so little borrowing, but the reason was plain to those on the inside. Killam was content to finance his companies internally, to nourish them with the profits they made. He had become, moreover, sceptical of new ideas.

Killam had never served on the boards of directors of companies other than his own, and it provoked comment and speculation. Nevertheless, in this his career did not change. Nor did he change his refusal to advise friends informally about investments, something he considered unwise.

But as he changed otherwise, as times changed, Royal Securities changed too. In the '30s the staff had argued that government bonds were safe bonds, especially attractive in an insecure world, and that they should be selling them. Killam agreed; they had the backing of the government, hence posed no direct responsibilities for him. He agreed when, from there, the firm wanted to go into the general bond business, then into municipal bonds. He agreed when after the war Montreal Engineering argued that it should be free to find work that had nothing to do with projects of his own. He agreed to Royal Securities' participation when the government in the '50s launched a "money market" by calling for weekly tenders on short-term treasury bills, a move that brought a whole new liquidity to the country's financial structure. The firm build up substantial inventories of the treasury bills and short-term government bonds, bought them, sold them and made money in the process. Its staff had argued, again, that it should buy a seat on the stock exchange and sell stocks and bonds like any brokerage house; as things had stood, for years it passed on customers' orders to other firms — which got the commission for the sales. This change, too, eventually came to pass in Killam's time. The unorthodox instrument he had wielded for his own designs had become an orthodox investment house, doing business from coast to coast, because he no longer dreamt the dreams that had made it otherwise.

There was change not only in him and in his company but in many things. The sort of federal budget of $37,000,000 that had exercised the Liberal press at the time of his birth became in his lifetime a laughable obscurity of history; Ottawa thought now in billions, and the billions kept growing. There was growth, too, of government regulation of finance, growth of social security, growth of the strength of labor, almost overwhelming growth of American investment in Canada, growth of a prosperous middle class that had money to invest, growth of the cities, growth of great new and impersonal collections of institutional investing power in the form of trust funds, mutual funds, pension funds, growth of a far wider range of securities on the market, growth of faceless corporations symbolized not by individualists like Beaverbrook and Killam and Sir Herbert Holt but by myriads of shareholders and by managers who came and went. Killam was becoming part of a thinning breed, the lonewolf promoter-builder.

And something else was vanishing too: the decades-old preeminence of St. James Street as the financial heart of the country. As Montreal financial columnist John Meyer saw it, The Street's fortunes had passed into second-generation money before Toronto showed real signs of developing capital on its own; it became debt-money, money more interested in security, in interest-paying things like bonds and mortgages than in the sort of risk investments that had made Killam wealthy. "There was a tendency," said Meyer, "to conserve it."

Toronto's Bay Street, on the other hand, was rising, was on the make, was more interested in speculation, and a postwar mining boom gave it impetus. St. James Street was more hesitant, it began to fall behind and Killam, in a sense, was

119

typical of what was happening; he didn't get into the mining boom. Apart from his age, he felt mining was something he knew too little about.

The process had gone on quietly, inexorably, almost imperceptibly but within a few years of the war Bay Street had taken the lead in equity investment, in risk capital, and within another 20 years it would be ahead in debt-money too. There were no documents to chronicle it, no proclamations to herald it, little public awareness, but an historic shift of power had taken place.

In 1950, at 65, Killam replied to a letter from an acquaintance. "I am not really carrying a tremendous load as you suggest," he said. "I fish all summer and swim all winter and most of my burdens are carried by others." He was a strong swimmer, a good waltzer — his sister said he'd always dance with the wallflowers — and he enjoyed both. As he changed with the years, he did take a lot more time for things like this, things other than business, for long winter holidays in Nassau, long summer holidays fishing salmon, for being with his wife. They spent on houses, on retinues of servants, on travel, on clothes, on entertainment, on fishing, on jewelry, on other things. If Killam sometimes hardly seemed to know what to do with his money, his wife had lavish tastes. To a doctor who knew her well, she was an 18th century woman who would have loved to live in the heyday of kings and courts and nobles with great castles. One of her favorite possessions was one of the seven Vigée-Lebrun paintings of Marie Antoinette. Said the doctor: "I always felt it symbolized her feeling for style and grandeur. It represented a sort of fulfillment." She kept it always in a prominent place, under the soft glow of a hidden light. She entertained in a manner which would today be considered exceptionally formal, liked to see people well dressed; their dinner guests usually came in evening dress and black or even white tie.

If she had expensive tastes, Killam liked to indulge them, especially during her long years of illness. She once told a friend they spent about $1,000,000 a year, and that long before inflation made a Disneyland of currency. She spent a lot on clothes. "She had masses of them... She had good taste.

Her clothes were out of this world." She took them with her in mounds of luggage which made her travels a celebrated facet of her panache. When she and a friend went once on a weekend visit, the friend took two valises, Mrs. Killam fifteen. When she went on longer trips, she took servants with her, all first class, and the movement of their baggage became a major operation. She also liked to take her dogs first class as well, and the time would come when she would engage in warfare against what is now Air Canada because they wouldn't let her. On one occasion she did get her two dogs — and servants — into the first class compartment. When she resisted having the dogs removed, the airline people transferred the passengers to another plane and flew them off, leaving her to fume to her entourage. Killam was just as happy if he could avoid this sort of thing. He was happier than she was, too, with their Montreal home, a spacious, well-appointed home with beautiful Victorian furnishings, with lovely old mahogany, a priceless collection of Waterford glass, good porcelain, good silver, crystal wall sconces.

Here Dorothy Killam presided over a household staff of some 10 people who liked both their work and their employers. "We stayed," said one of them, "as long as we could." They were devoted in particular to Mrs. Killam, and she to them. If they fell ill, she and her husband saw that they got the best medical care, visited them in hospital. If she had to pick a new servant, she did it with care. The servants were predominantly British, and the household was run, as one servant put it, "in the English style." The butler was the chief of staff. The lady's maid, Elizabeth MacDonald, ranked next and she held a special place indeed. If Mrs. Killam was a sort of mother to the servants, "MacDonald" was a sort of firm older aunt to Dorothy Killam — servant, close personal friend and occasional critic combined. She didn't hesitate to chide her lady if she felt it was required. "Now stop that nonsense," she'd say in her Scots' burr. She came to Mrs. Killam just after her marriage and was with her when she died — over 40 years later.

There were always dogs around. Killam sometimes took one of them on his drive to the office, and would pat it affectionately when he got out. Sometimes he would take one to romp on Mount Royal while he sat, all by himself, on a bench overlooking Beaver Lake.

121

The Montreal home, said a friend, "was old fashioned and comfortable. It was Killam." They also had two winter homes in Nassau, one bought in the '30s, the second in the '40s. The first was next door to the governor's residence, an expensively revamped version of a structure once occupied by British Army officers and including former slave quarters. When the Duke and Duchess of Windsor were ensconced next door they became friends, with a gate between the two estates to handle the considerable traffic of their neighborliness. "If Wally had too many guests, she would send some of them over to Dorothy." The second house, on the former estate of U.S. aluminum tycoon Arthur Vining Davis, was on Hog (now Paradise) Island, about a mile across the water. Guests might lunch at one, have dinner at the other.

In these tropical homes, set beside a turquoise sea, the Killams mixed with conservative members of the international set that frequented the Bahamas, largely American and British men who had made their mark in the worlds of finance, business or politics. They entertained elegantly and superbly, usually for small, select groups but occasionally with many guests sitting down to candle-lit dinners indoors or out on the lawns among the gracious trees and flowers of the southern seas.

"Dorothy's parties," said one who knew from experience, "were exquisite," her tables a mirror of splendor and of her very considerable talents as an organizer. She was not only a good manager herself, she always had an excellent butler to make sure that things went well because they were prepared well.

She herself was the centre of the stage. There had been a time, a long time, after her cancer operations when she was depressed and withdrawn, convinced that her life was over. But when that passed "she was like a liberated child," and not even the chronic pain and difficulties of her arthritis stayed her. Nervous, frail now, high-strung, at times imperious, she could light up a room, and she knew it. She was theatrical and vibrantly alive, a woman who could sew so well that some said she could have made a living at it, who liked both jazz and opera, who smoked "like a chimney" but quit completely when it threatened her health, who could speak French and

German passably well, who could spend hours on the telephone. "She liked to stamp things with her own personality," and her personality was reflected in the jewelry she wore. She accumulated a valuable collection of it, one worth millions.

One piece included a diamond that weighed 39.21 carats. She had the pearls John Jacob Astor had snatched up hurriedly as the *Titanic* sank and thrown down to his wife in a lifeboat while he remained behind to die; the huge Briolet diamond which had belonged to King Henri II of France. She wore the Briolet diamond as a pendant suspended on a slim diamond chain. She wore bracelets which a friend once tried on and found as "heavy as handcuffs." They weighted 302 carats. She wore her jewelry frequently and in many places, at balls, parties, the opera, even at their fishing camp. When a jeweller suggested that he should make her imitations for use in public, she scorned the idea. She bought diamonds, she said, to wear.

They could transform her into sheer spectacle, as three executives of a Killam company saw one evening. They were in the Montreal living room, having a drink, when one of them saw her descending the stairs. He caught his breath. Diamonds glittered from her hair, her ears, her wrists, from her long-sleeved black dress. At dinner they flirted a psychedelic radiance into the candlelight.

Yet perhaps because one of the guests seemed unimpressed, Mrs. Killam held up her bracelet and said it was caught in her sleeve. She asked him to help free it. He did but even from that close range remained non-committal. So she asked him what he thought of the things she wore.

"Very nice," he said.

"They're real, you know," she drawled.

Killam liked to poke fun at her whims. When she redecorated the living room of their Montreal home in striking black and white decor, his comment was that it would be a good place for a skating party. When she wanted to keep abreast of current and cultural events, he hired a university professor to coach her, then would ask about her "tooter." But he didn't joke about her yen for jewelry. In his devotion to her, he was happy to buy whatever she wanted but he also had another motive. He once told colleagues he could think of no better hedge against economic ups and downs than diamonds. Having made that decision, he did a characteristic thing. He got to know a lot about them.

An executive at Montreal's fashionable Henry Birks & Co. said both Killams would come into the store to buy but that it was Killam who knew most about the subject. She knew style. He went beyond that. "He was nobody to tell little white lies to. He knew too much. He liked jewelry personally and he came to know more about it than most of our salesmen. He knew stones. He'd ask us to keep an eye out for something, or we might call him and say we had something he might want to see. He wanted records for anything he bought, and he'd be let down if she was disappointed in his selection. And selection wasn't easy. She had everything — brooches, rings, necklaces, everything."

Killam indulged his wife in a second interest — baseball. "She had it," said a friend, "on the brain." She had been keen about the game since her youth when she used to go out to Sportsman's Park to watch the Browns. "They were the favorite team in St. Louis then," she once told a reporter. "George Sisler was their star, and folks in St. Louis thought he was bigger than either Ty Cobb or Babe Ruth."

In Montreal she became a fan of the Royals, top farm team of the Brooklyn Dodgers, liked to go with friends to their games in the east end's Delormier Stadium; there she saw Jackie Robinson become the first black to break into organized baseball. Indeed, there is one story that years before the advent of today's Expos Killam had inquiries made about the possibility of buying the stadium and enlarging it for a major league franchise.

Nothing came of that. Instead, it was the Dodgers themselves who became the ultimate focus of Mrs. Killam's baseball interest. It started in the '40s when business frequently took her husband to New York. He would come to share some of her feeling for the Dodgers, but colleagues doubt that his interest approached hers. Hers grew into outright devotion though one sportswriter was impious enough to suggest that her enthusiasm was probably rooted in "her rich sense of humor." Her own explanation was that she was "impressed by the Dodgers' terrific desire to win and the extreme loyalty of the colorful Brooklyn fans." There may be a link between the two descriptions in the rise of what were once known as The Bums, a screwball team, from the implausible, the zany, to the imperial, the excellent.

Killam was glad to see her so interested, especially when she was ill. When she was confined to the house during one world series, he had a special television cable brought in at considerable expense so she could watch the games in a Montreal then without TV.

She once told a reporter it was originally Killam's idea to try to buy the Brooklyn team. Killam's sister said "Walton told her he'd buy it if she tried harder to get well. He was enthralled by her interest." But in a later conversation with her lawyer, Mrs. Killam indicated it was more or less of a joke. She said he came back to their New York hotel one day, said the Dodgers might be for sale and asked if she'd like to buy them. She said they both laughed it off. But if she wasn't serious then the indications are that she became more so later.

Killam had a very real respect for his wife's judgment and opinions, especially those concerning people. If he wanted to get a reading on someone, he would ask her to sit next to that guest at dinner and then report her opinion later. "She had," said a friend, "an almost infallible eye for spotting character and she took pride in it. She judged a person not so much by what he said but by his reaction to things, and in my experience and opinion she was never wrong."

Killam's respect for her went beyond that. Night after night for years in the library of the Montreal home he would spread out his papers and "think out loud" about his problems. Mrs. Killam would listen, and respond to an occasional question or sometimes ask a question of her own. He was schooling her for a future when he wouldn't be around, when she would have control of the empire he had built and the millions he had made. He found her an apt pupil. He once told someone she had the best business brain of any woman he ever met.

14

THE GENEROUS

TIGHTWAD

One day a visitor was in the handsome office of one of the big men in the Montreal financial world. They were interrupted by a call from a financial man of comparable note. The telephone conversation stirred the host to repeated expressions of delight. He couldn't be more pleased, and he wanted the caller to know it. The visitor was convinced that he was witnessing the reaction of a man to news that he had made a lot of money. But it wasn't that at all. The caller had said he had just succeeded in getting a large donation to a charity in which they were mutually interested.

In the upper reaches of the capitalist world this sort of thing goes on all the time — big men ranging among their peers on behalf of all sorts of funds, drives, campaigns. They grumble about it but they do it. It is accepted as one of the burdens, and one of the badges, of wealth and position.

Izaak Walton Killam never fitted into this pattern any more easily than he did into others; as his wealth grew people talked about him not so much because he had made so much money but because they considered he gave so little away. One Montreal businessman said he went to him to raise money for a charity and that Killam made it perfectly and quickly clear that he was wasting the time of both of them. Attempts to get him to give to things in Yarmouth got nowhere. When an attempt was made in Montreal to get him to make a large contribution to a proposed cultural showplace, he said he didn't believe in giving for the construction of buildings; they didn't last and, moreover, if people wanted support for a project they should at least be able to build it. One noted businessman said he never got far with Killam either. "Whenever I visited him," he said, "my mission was to obtain a contribution from him or Royal Securities for some worthy cause. My experience was that contributions were always small in relation to expectations."

The truth appears to be that Killam did give to good causes, though never in particularly large amounts relative to his wealth. This, however, wasn't too unusual. If Killam's gifts were meagre, one businessman said, so were those of "many successful men of that period."

Because his records are gone there is no way of telling exactly how much he gave and to whom and what. But one of his former secretaries said that Killam donated considerable sums every year to charitable causes, to universities, hospitals. The cut-off guideline was usually the amount he could claim as an income tax exemption. Mrs. Killam, in turn, once said her husband gave far more than he ever got credit for.

Is so, the fault was typically his own. He either channelled gifts through others or, if he gave directly, he insisted on anonymity. He gave to the Montreal Children's Hospital and, contrary to a belief that he never served any institution outside his own business, he worked on a key committee of its board for some years, giving advice on financial matters. Records of at least four universities indicate that he contributed to them.

He gave with his eyes wide open. When Halifax's Dalhousie University bestowed on him the honorary degree of doctor of laws in 1948, a colleague's wife called to congratulate him. His response was: "You know why they did it" — though he seemed pleased when she said she was happy for him anyway. Dalhousie extolled him as "one of the most distinguished Nova Scotians in the financial life of the Dominion and a man who has displayed the same courage and skill as was shown by his ancestors in the previous century." But they had a hard time to get him to have his picture taken, and Killam rejected other such overtures, two by one Maritime university.

127

The signs were that he wasn't bothered if he was called a tightwad. A friend said "he didn't give a hoot what people thought of him." Someone else said he would even chuckle about it. Some thought his attitude was shaped not only by his own character but by unhappy experiences in Yarmouth and Monteal, and by incidents such as one in which he was said to have donated a downtown Montreal site for headquarters for a certain organization, then reacted in anger when they sold it at a profit. Perhaps, too, there was another factor: he knew, if many others didn't, the numerous quiet kindnesses he did and the sentiment he could feel. They stood in contrast to his general reputation.

It had been said on The Street, yes, that he and Ward Pitfield never spoke after their 1928 split. Not so, said Arthur Torrey who left Royal Securities with Pitfield and eventually headed the Pitfield company. When Pitfield became seriously ill in the '30s, Torrey said, Killam came to see him, became solicitious; he was even said to have offered the doctors, the hospital money if money would work a cure. Pitfield told Torrey they had patched up their differences, that they were going to work together when he got well. He never did.

It was Torrey who eventually made what could have been seen as a symbolic gesture to heal the wound. For years, he'd say, he'd regretted the split, and in 1948 he went to Killam to propose a merger of Royal Securities and what had become Pitfield, MacKay & Co. Ltd. "He asked for our balance sheet," Torrey said, "studied it, and said, 'You've done very well, better than we have recently.'" But, he added, he didn't think it would be fair for him, at 63, to make such a decision; he'd leave it to vice president Albert Culver. When Torrey finally got his answer it was "no."

But it was in another episode that Killam's sentiment again came out. In the '50s his fishing camp burned down and when one of his executives, Mowbray Jones, son of The Colonel, came for a visit the ruins were still there. Jones was poking around them one day when something golden caught his eye. He dug it out and took it to Killam.

Killam stared at it, identified it. It was, he said, the gift Pitfield had given him and Dorothy on their wedding day. He was, said Jones, obviously deeply moved to get it back.

Killam once met a man from Yarmouth who had taught him in school but became unemployed. Killam said he was just the man he was seeking for Mersey Paper, and made a job for him. He gave jobs to various relatives. He put on the lists of the fund he stowed away for employees a member of the staff who hailed from Yarmouth and who had a talent for picking the wrong stocks to buy. When a lowly employee found it difficult to run errands any longer, Killam gave him a sedentary job, visited him at his home for chats. When the man's daughter was about to be married, he confessed to Killam that she had always dreamt of going to the church in a Rolls Royce. She went in Killam's Rolls Royce. His kindnesses to people in hospital were legion. He once gave money to a needy acquaintance who drank too much; he didn't repeat it — because the man kept on drinking. He gave to an old ladies home in Yarmouth at a time when an elderly relative was living there. He helped members of his household staff and their families out of various troubles. He saw that salaries were paid for years to a fair number of employees who, for one reason or another, could no longer work. In his family, he was a generous son and brother; among other kindnesses, he gave his mother and sisters very large gifts indeed.

The sisters were a stark contrast. One was the effervescent, radiant Elizabeth Rodgers, the other the shy, quiet, indrawn Connie Killam who made one think, years after he'd gone, that in her one was seeing what he himself had been like.

They sat with the writer for hours one day in their home outside Boston, and Elizabeth chattered pleasantly on and on. But occasionally she'd pause and say, "Connie, I'm tired of talking. Now you say something."

"Tea?" Connie would say, and that was all.

"Well," said Elizabeth after one such episode, "I'll tell you a story about Walton and Connie. He came to visit us, and he got around to seeing what Connie was doing with her money. She brought him some documents, and he studied them. Then he called her upstairs and said, 'Connie, you are investing your money in stocks. I didn't give it to you to take risks with.'

"So she stood there, embarrassed, and he wanted to know where she was investing it, and she said with a brokerage

129

firm in Boston. He was thinking that over when she said, 'all right then, Walton, I'll sell the stocks.' "

" 'Oh, no,' he said. 'Don't sell them. They're good stocks, and that's a good company.' "

Perhaps it had shaken him that she, like himself, liked to do things in her own way. And the simple explanation appears to be that Killam gave but, characteristically, he preferred to do it in his own way. He didn't like being compared to others. He didn't like being pushed. He liked having his own ideas. Perhaps his wife reflected his viewpoint in telling of a case in which a university representative sought money from her. "He tried," she stormed, "to tell me what to do with my money." A certain delicacy, said her lawyer, was imperative in the approach. "There can be subtle differences between telling and quietly raising the possibility, and this man did it the wrong way." He went away with nothing.

There was one further aspect of Killam's giving that Mrs. Killam once raised. She said he had a long-range plan for his money after death just as he always had a long-range plan for his money in life.

A lot of his attitude in life is crystallized in the Harry Bell story. Bell was an engineer with Montreal Engineering, and a close relative of Killam. He was the son of Dr. Jane Heartz Bell who practised medicine in Halifax for many years and who once took in an ill young Walton Killam and nursed him back to health. He never forgot.

When Harry Bell fell ill with multiple sclerosis Killam paid his salary for more than a quarter of a century, and he used to go out to the Bell home in the suburban Town of Mount Royal, especially when Dr. Bell came to town. Harry Bell's wife said he liked to sit around chatting about family matters: "We treated him as just another member of the family, and he liked it. He'd sit on the living-room chesterfield, his finger playing with a hole in the slipcover." Sometimes he'd ask her, as a nurse, to take his blood pressure. During the war when they had no car, he put one at their disposal. To Mrs. Bell, he was "a fabulous man, quite different from his public image."

It was, in turn, Bell's illness which became a factor in the Killams' fascinating ties with the Montreal Neurological

Institute, a medical establishment made world famous by the great brain surgeon, Dr. Wilder Penfield, and his staff.

They became over the years part of its tapestry of talk. One of its doctors became Mrs. Killam's family physician and was until her death. Another designed a small therapeutic swimming pool for their basement to help her fight arthritis. Mrs. Killam eventually had to have nurses with her much of the time, and she liked to have Montreal Neurological Institute nurses. She took an interest in their work, and was a patient at the Institute too. Miss Eileen Flanagan, its forthright director of nursing, liked both Killams. She said Killam once slipped quietly into her office and asked if she needed anything for the wards. Miss Flanagan said they could use some television sets. Five showed up next morning, with no explanation of who had sent them.

Some time after it was founded in 1934 as an offshoot of McGill University, Killam had become interested in the Institute's work. When one of his New Brunswick fishing guides fell ill, Killam had him brought to the Institute at his own expense and, as usual, showed concern over his progress. Dr. William Cone, Penfield's buoyant, dynamic, right-hand man, operated on the patient and refused to take a fee. Killam became intrigued by his work, and Cone became a friend of both him and his wife.

When Bell came down with the disease, Killam became interested in the battle against multiple sclerosis. Eventually he asked Dr. Penfield if the Institute would undertake a research program into it if he gave $50,000. Penfield wasn't too interested in adding this to an already heavy workload, but he agreed to do it. Killam gave the $50,000 anonymously in 1949 and a research project was launched which went on for years, with the Killam money providing part of the financing.

That was Killam's idea. Then that same year Penfield had one of his own. The institute badly needed money for a new wing, so he went to the gray stone house on Sherbrooke street to do what he often had to do. "I was," he'd say with a wry smile in his 80s, "a beggar for years." This time his target was $1,000,000.

He outlined the Institute's problems and suggested a Killam endowment fund or foundation. Killam showed a lot of interest and did promise some help. Then finally, pushed too far, he blew up and said *he* would decide what to do with his money.

"I have never," Penfield recalled years later, "been treated so rudely or abruptly in my life."

Later that year Killam tried to soothe him in two ways. A large salmon arrived at the Penfield home with the name I. Killam scrawled on the crate. Then Killam sent the Institute $50,000 from himself and $30,000 from companies he controlled. Both, he stipulated, were to be kept anonymous.

The last letter on the file Penfield kept of their correspondence was dated Jan. 14, 1954, and concerned the work the Institute had done on multiple sclerosis. It was continuing, Penfield wrote, and some of it had been brilliant.

It didn't save Harry Bell. The disease eventually killed him.

15

DEATH BESIDE

THE RIVER

The May 29, 1951, issue of Beaverbrook's London *Evening Standard* chronicled a milestone in Killam's life. It noted that he had just sold one of his properties and that "it is the first time this little-known man has realized assets built on a lifelong faith in the future of Canada's forests." It complimented the 65-year-old Killam for his vision in seeing "the green gold" of Canada as the key to success which had made him "perhaps the richest man in Canada."

"He hated to sell things," a colleague said. "It was as though he would have to part with a bit of his life." But now he had sold British Columbia Pulp and Paper to Abitibi, and the fact that he did so showed how the waters ran in the tides of that life.

His cousin Lawrence, Killam once said, had tackled "perhaps the heaviest load" he had laid on anyone in running the company. Its mills, its logging camps, its operations were an important facet in the province's forest industry but they had never ranked among the best of their kind, had never undergone drastic modernization. But in the post-war years the firm's production of high-grade bleached sulphite pulp made it a highly profitable business, so much so that American companies began to eye it in their desire to build themselves into the structure of a thriving Canadian Pacific coast. But

Killam had never wanted his possessions to pass into American hands, had said so and meant it. He fended them off.

Even so, Canada's Abitibi Pulp and Paper Company picked up rumors that Killam had given someone an option to buy. With Pacific coast aspirations of its own, Abitibi set up a meeting with Killam and was told he had given no option to anybody. But he did name a figure at which he'd be willing to sell to Abitibi. They bought, and Killam then did something which became part of the tales told about him by Andrew Armstrong, a courtly Irishman who came to head that branch of Royal Securities which bought and sold securities.

Armstrong had tremendous admiration for Killam: "He had more brains than the rest of them put together. And he had guts." And, he said, when Killam sold B.C. Pulp he immediately instructed his trader to place a bid for some of its stock at the share price he had been paid, one well above the market price. "It was a signal," Armstrong said. "He had owned most of the stock but he wanted to let smaller shareholders know what they should be able to get."

Killam did get for the company far more than it had cost him, and what he did with the money was not what he would have done in the past. He did not reinvest the proceeds — he put them in the bank. The reason appears to be that he was no longer interested in further investments. He was worrying now, instead, about the size of the estate he would leave his wife and what he should do about it. And what he did about that estate is, in a sense, the ultimate paradox in a paradoxical life.

He didn't like taxes. Despite his 1917 plea to the government for comprehensive wartime financial measures, despite his criticism of the belated imposition of an income tax, this remained true till the day he died. One Montreal lwayer said he handled the negotiations for Killam's purchase of a fishing camp in the '50s and that, when he sent his bill in, Killam blew up over a single item, a tiny transfer tax: "I had a hard time getting him off the phone." He probably disliked taxes for a variety of reasons. More than once he said he'd worked all his life; perhaps he was human enough to want the fruits of his toil for himself and not for others. He had grown up in a society in which taxes were virtually irrelevant; he was

32 by the time an income tax came in, 42 when corporate dividends became taxable. As taxation went on from there to become a creeping labyrinth, he reacted. To some extent, he had apprehensions about the welfare state which ate up so much money, felt it would blunt initiative; he was willing to help those in trouble but he had the self-made man's conviction that people should stand on their own feet.

It was to some extent this attitude which led him to minimize for years the payment of dividends from the earnings of his own companies. In an era when there was no impost on capital gains, he preferred to keep the money in a company's treasury to finance growth or maintenance, to provide working capital, to enhance its value. "What sense does it make to pay dividends," he was quoted as saying, "when you have to turn around and borrow to do things?" There came a time at the annual meeting of one of his companies when, it is said, one small shareholder cried out against such policies. "It's all right for you if you don't pay dividends," he complained to Killam. "You're a rich man but I'm not. I need the money." But there weren't enough small shareholders to bother Killam too much. He liked at least 70% control, and in most cases he had it.

There were other aspects to all this. When Newfoundland joined Canada in 1949 he took his Newfoundland Light and Power Company out of the orbit of International Power to avoid the risks of making that parent holding company taxable in Canada. At least once he used his no-dividends policy as a weapon in negotiations with a large company interested in a deal with Calgary Power. When it came to bargaining over financial terms, Killam blandly noted that Calgary Power hadn't paid dividends in years. He turned to Geoffrey Gaherty. "We're impoverished," he said, "aren't we Gaherty? Impoverished!"

It was said on The Street that Killam annually spent many hours arranging his affairs so that he would be meticulously within the law yet pay the minimum possible level of taxation. Yet his attitude could reflect the paradoxes of his character: a lawyer said he once pointed out to Ottawa a tax loophole that should be plugged.

It was against this background that he faced the final confrontation with this fiscal monster which had grown up in

135

his lifetime. Lawyers reminded him more than once of a fact he knew all too well: that his estate would be heavily taxed unless he did something about it. He could do something about it by, say, establishing a foundation to channel much of his money to worthy causes. He did consider a foundation. He did, in one of several wills, provide that if his wife predeceased him his estate would go to charities. But he never got around to stipulating what charities.

He was tired and sick and he told his wife it had become too much for him to make such decisions. He abandoned any idea of making a complicated will. He told Mrs. Killam that he had made his money largely in Canada and that he wanted it to go back to the Canadian people, that he was going to leave everything to her and that she could then write the will they had talked over together. He had schooled her in handling money, given her the broad outlines of his own thought. She could decide precisely what to do once he was gone.

One cabinet minister in later years said Killam told him he realized Ottawa would take a large bite out of his estate but that he was convinced it was right to let it happen. "I hope the money will be put to good use," he was quoted as saying, "but you people know more about that than I do."

It was an old man's acceptance of one of the phenomena of the era, the ever-growing role of government in Canadian society.

One night at his fishing lodge, late in Killam's life, he fell to talking with Dr. G.R. Brow, a leading Montreal heart specialist, one of several doctors who passed through the Killam experience, who knew them both in those long years when the husband brooded over the health of his wife and the wife watched his like a hawk. Brow had his own memories of what it could be like. He could recall one Christmas Eve when he got a call from Nassau: Mrs. Killam said she'd like him to come, with two nurses, because her husband was ill.

Brow was a calm and gathered man by nature, and it was just as well. For it was a stormy day, and there were no flights to Nassau. Yet by night he had cancelled his own Christmas plans, appealed all the way up to the president of the then Trans-Canada Air Lines, been provided with a special plane and crew, rummaged around and found two nurses. They took off in swirling snow. When they got to Nassau he found that Killam would survive. He spent Christmas there, in an elaborate home where by custom everyone gathered around the tree for an exchange of gifts and the white servants served dinner to the black.

Now, not long after but on a quiet summer's night in a northern forest with the river trysting to the sea outside the door, Brow sat talking to Killam in his fishing lodge. He was there to look after him. He'd looked after a lot of big men in his time and it didn't bother him. He could relax with them. He could see the vaguely uncomfortable realities behind the unreal public images. He was, moreover, the sort of doctor, the sort of easy man people do talk to, and Killam this night was no exception.

The doctor had grown up in Prince Edward Island and they found themselves yarning about their native Maritime Provinces, yarning with the blend of affection and pride and regret that is common to their expatriates. Killam had said more than once that it saddened him that so many people had to leave there to make a living, and he knew the reason as well as any man. He talked about their economy, the crux of it all. What it needed, he said, was the stimulation, the reinforcement of cheap power, and he felt science had at last found the key in atomic energy. He was thinking, he said, of building a nuclear power plant along the eastern seaboard.

It was the sort of vision that had made him rich, and it didn't stand alone. One day about the same time Killam walked into the Canadian Embassy in Washington to see its Counsellor, Robert Farquharson, his last managing editor on the *Mail and Empire*. He was thinking, he said, of trying to buy the *Globe and Mail* and he wondered if Farquharson would become his publisher if he did. Farquharson said he'd be glad to.

These were visions, dreams, but fragile, abortive echoes of the kind that once had flourished in a great constructive mind. The strength was no longer there to make them more. When Farquharson heard next from Killam it was a note from someone else: he'd had to abandon his plans. He was ill.

In late January 1954 the Montreal *Gazette* reported a "terse, unembroidered announcement of changes among the top executives of Royal Securities." After 39 years, Killam was stepping down as president though he remained a director of Royal Securities and other companies as well as chairman of Calgary Power's board. H.J. Symington had also resigned as vice president and A.F. Culver had become president.

The story was written by Associate Editor Guy S. Cunliffe, ironically the former *Mail and Empire* reporter who had been sent that day in 1936 to cover the baleful story of that paper's sale. He had praise for Killam: "one of the most outstanding and successful (but least publicized) figures in the Canadian financial world." In the past half-century, he said, "with Mr. Killam's hand ever close upon the helm, Royal Securities has taken an active and often dominating part, not only in the financing but also in the organization (or reorganization) of numerous enterprises, especially in the pulp and paper industry and the electric power development field. The continuing, profitable success of such undertakings constitutes a collective monument to his quiet but penetrating discernment, and the shrewd skill of his judgment."

Now Killam had decided to retire and to offer Royal Securities and its related Montreal Engineering operation to the senior members of his staff. The terms were liberal and payment of the balance of price was extended over several years. Said Denis Stairs: "He practically gave Montreal Engineering to us. He even offered to lend us the money to buy it."

Three months after the announcement of his retirement, Killam was a patient in New York's Presbyterian Hospital after what he called "a mild heart attack." In late May he wrote a friend that "I am convalescing slowly and I hope satisfactorily. I may be able to get away shortly for my summer's fishing."

It was fishing, a number of people said, that kept him going as his health flagged in his late 60s. He looked forward as eagerly as his namesake Izaak Walton ever had to the arrival of word in May that the salmon were running. "He just had to go fishing," a colleague said. "That's what saved his life."

It was fishing, too, that gave rise to one of numerous pieces of misinformation about him: it was said in print more than once that he was an ardent angler who never caught a fish.

In fact, he caught a lot of them. He could catch them where others couldn't. He was an excellent fisherman, and he became one in a typical way. He studied it. He had an original edition of Walton's *The Compleat Angler*, his sister Elizabeth said, and he read it numerous times. He studied the factors that brought angling success: the habits of salmon, the waters where they lurked, the use of flies, other things. Unlike his father, he didn't tie his own flies but he had a lot of them, and knew the significance of them. One night in Montreal he took whole trays of them out to show Mrs. Rodgers.

He fished in many places, on business trips to the west coast, on the east coast, elsewhere. One April when he was visiting Liverpool, he said he'd like to try the Mersey. It was a bleak, cold day but nothing would stop him. Men watched in wonder from the shore as he sat in a small boat, a silent, pale, white-haired man in a light coat with a half-frozen guide behind him, trying without success to hook a salmon.

But it was in northern New Brunswick and Quebec's neighboring Gaspe that he fished most, on majestic rivers that laugh through rugged hills, rivers almost as pristine, as beautiful yet as at the time they were created. They were the haunts of rich and privileged men, and it was rich and privileged men who kept them that way. They controlled them, and protected them.

Killam was one of them for years. In 1928 a press report said he owned some of the best fishing waters on the Restigouche River. In 1940 he had widened his activities by joining the exclusive Ristigouche Salmon Club, with headquarters at Matapedia, Que., and a membership limited to 20. He was for some time its only Canadian member.

Sometimes he thought while he sat in the canoe, with a guide casting. Sometimes he read a whodunit. He had a doctor and a nurse with him much of the time in his last years, and sometimes he defied their orders in going fishing at all. One day when a doctor told him he shouldn't, he found his own solution: he took the doctor with him. Once when a nurse advised him to stay in bed, he waited till she had gone to make a long-distance call some miles away, then got up and went to the river; without Killam's knowledge, the nurse had been instructed by Mrs. Killam to report to her every day on her husband's condition.

139

His passion for fishing merged with his passion for detail in the record book he kept for years. It chronicled not only every salmon killed in his waters but who had caught it, the time of day, the weather, the fly used, every conceivable factor. It amazed visitors.

In the early '50s he widened his activities again. He purchased a camp on Quebec's Grand Cascapedia River, one of the three enclaves in a private compound. He bought it from Americans and he bought it, colleagues say, because the Cascapedia then was said to yield the greatest salmon killed on the continent. It drew the aging Killam like a magnet; before he died he wanted to try his skills against the biggest and the best.

His main lodge burnt down not long after he bought it. He and a doctor were lucky to get out in their pyjamas, and his record book went up in the flames. It didn't stop his fishing. He moved into the guest house and went right on.

Despite his heart attack earlier that year, he never fished more or harder than he did in 1954. He killed many salmon, big salmon, one of 42 pounds, one of 43, one of 45, friends say, and in keeping with time-honoured ritual the silhouettes of all three were traced on boards which were hung on a wall for all to see. He was so proud of the biggest that he kept it intact until it began to stink.

He was back again in 1955. In August a friend came down to join him, and after lunch on the 5th Killam told him he had had a lovely time out on the river that morning but that he was tired now and thought he'd have a nap. When he'd gone in to lie down, his nurse left to phone in her report on his health to Mrs. Killam. When she came back, his heart had stopped.

Not too long before he died he'd been sitting around the camp talking to that old colleague and admirer, Denis Stairs, a man who in all their years together had never called him anything but Mr. Killam. He told about a woman he had known in his youth, a good woman he wanted to help because she needed it. But she was too proud to accept help from him, so he had to find another way. He did at last get it to her, through his sisters. He chuckled as he told how it had all worked out, and the chuckle was like the rustle of dry leaves.

16

REBUKE, PRAISE,

SURPRISE

The immediate effect of Killam's death was a focusing on the dimensions of his mystery. A group of Montreal newspaper reporters were having a drink when one of them mentioned his passing. "Killam," someone said, "who was he?" Even a Nova Scotian in the group didn't know. In its story the Canadian Press, the national news agency, gave a partial answer: "A mystery man to the public but a power behind the scenes in Canadian finance."

The problem was that the press knew little more about him than the public, and the public knew little or nothing at all. Said *Time*: "The muted coverage of his death in Montreal's newspapers would have satisfied even Killam's passion for obscurity. The most recent photograph of him was 10 years old. Newspaper files were almost bare of information. The Montreal *Gazette* ran a 36-line obituary on an inside page while the *Star* could muster only 20 sentences." *Time* had asked its Nova Scotia correspondent to file a report from Halifax; Harold Shea was amazed to find so few people who knew anything about Killam in the province where he'd been born, where he'd invested in numerous concerns, and where in recent years he'd liked to go on long car drives, admiring the mellow beauties of its landscape.

Some papers used the picture of him that had been dug out of Toronto *Daily Star* files in 1927. It was all they had. The editor of Montreal's weekly *Financial Times* knew so little about Killam that he asked Royal Securities' C.H. Link to write an editorial on him. Like those which eventually appeared in the city's *Star* and *Gazette*, it was a conventional eulogy of a capitalist paper for a capitalist giant. It praised his vision, his courage, his contribution to Canada, his skill in financial promotion and as a "doctor of companies." The *Star* said his passing "will leave a large gap in the industrial and financial life of the country." The *Gazette* said his life "strikingly demonstrated the opportunities for progress Canada holds for her sons." It praised his "vision, confidence and persistence," his recovery from Riordon. "He started with little; he achieved much; he successfully met tremendous reverses and overcame great obstacles." His was a career, added the *Gazette*, "that might have been much more spectacular and better known had it not been for a characteristic reticence. This was a trait which was particularly noticeable in connection with his considerable philanthropies, among which the Children's Memorial Hospital was prominent."

It remained for the weekly tabloid *Midnight*, hardly a conservative publication, to pen the warmest eulogy. In a two-part article, it said Killam "had more money than Little Orphan Annie's Daddy Warbucks — and that's plenty!" Its stories, it confessed, "would have made Ike spin." One said Max Aitken had originally hired him in Halifax because Aitken "had the face of a friendly gorilla" and he figured that "a good-looking guy could help him meet the gals." But Killam told him "I am not interested in them at all. I just think about money." So they set out to make their fortunes together.

Midnight said Killam "hated to be asked for money. He nearly flipped. But when any charity drive was about to fail bankers could call him for a big check. He gave anonymously, and sometimes through other persons. He had tremendous faith in Canada, God, and most of all in the power and influence of money."

The final story ended by saying: "The Good Book says that it is easier for a camel to go through the eye of a needle than for a rich man to go into heaven. However Ike has a record of making history." He had come from obscure origins and he had become rich, yes, but he "pumped that money into management, into the growth of our country. He made money come to life, work, and grow, for he had tremendous faith in its power for good. Ike Killam, virtually unknown by the majority of Canadians, the richest man in the land till his heart stopped, leaves behind him a monument to his modesty in the form of sound, powerful, thriving business enterprise. Ike has a good chance to beat the prediction of the Good Book."

Others were less charitable. When word got out that, apart from succession duties, Killam had left everything to his wife there were harsh things said in Montreal and elsewhere. Hospitals, universities, other institutions that had hoped for bequests knew now there would be none. The Street came up with one more apocryphal anecdote, this time about Killam's funeral. As the procession filed towards Mount Royal Cemetery, it was said, there was a traffic jam and by the time it was unsnarled a Brinks truck had joined the mourners. "See," said a man in one of the cars, "I told you: he *is* going to take it with him."

The attitude eventually found its way into an editorial in the *Financial Post* after the death on January 1, 1956, of another Maritime-born giant, Sir James Dunn. It was headed "Wealth Has Its Uses and Its Obligations." It named neither man but it was dated March 10, 1956, and its intent was obvious. It noted that one "forceful developer" — Dunn — had died without leaving any of his $70,000,000 estate to any public cause. It added:

> There does not seem to have been any public release of news about the estate of another wealthy Canadian financier who died recently after a lifetime of creating wealth, accumulating wealth and hanging on to what he made. But it is pretty well established that his estate exceeded $200,000,000 and that nothing whatever was left to any public philanthropy, hospital, educational institution or cultural enterprise.

These are unusual examples. Most wealthy men today are generous in their lives and in their wills. Many give freely to a wide variety of socially useful projects

143

. . .Some give or leave money to foundations . . . The social good worked by these foundations is in remarkable contrast to the selfishness of the few wealthy men who cannot bring themselves to spare a dime.

Of course, the men of wealth who did not give generously in their lifetimes or at the time of their death make their contribution anyway. Death taxes look after that. It is perhaps a legitimate approach to the problem for a man to argue that he can save himself a lot of trouble by not deciding who is going to get the benefit of his money on a tax-free basis. "Let the government take its share when I die," he may say, "and give it to hospitals, schools, etc." As a matter of fact, the owner of the $200 million estate was once heard to say that this was the fairest as well as the easiest solution.

But it is a solution that lacks a social sense and it certainly suggests that the individual's imagination stopped short at money-making and did not extend into the uses and obligations of wealth.

The *Financial Post's* estimate of the value of the Dunn estate was a bit high. It was much further out in estimating Killam's but then so were many others. It came, according to a legal firm involved, to $83,000,000. No figure appears to have been made public on the exact amount of death taxes exacted from these two estates, but it was about half the total in each case.

Once the initial flurry of interest died away, no one would talk much about Killam for years. When Peter Newman published his study of Canadian financial and economic giants called *Flame of Power* in 1959, some people were surprised that it had not a word about him. Explained Newman: "I simply couldn't dig up enough information about him."

But as former colleagues and others grew old they were willing, and even eager, to talk of the Killam they had known. It was noted, for one thing, that it was a striking fact that he had made not only himself but a substantial number of associates wealthy. He did it, in the opinion of Graham Towers, the notable first Governor of The Bank of Canada,

144

without being "a manipulator, a juggler of the market. He was absolutely honest, a long-term fellow who got companies going and took a continuing interest in them. He was, in my opinion, one of the most creative people Canada has ever had. He was a builder. Canada needs more men like him." Echoes Dr. John Bates, a man who knew, from years in the industry, as much about the story of the Canadian pulp and paper industry as anyone ever did: "This country is crying out for men like Killam. He was the ablest Canadian of his time, not just in business and finance, but in his concepts, in his ability to look years ahead. He wasn't a short-range, fast-buck boy. He created wealth. He foresaw things, and he stuck to them. You never heard of a Royal Securities come-on. Killam created solid things that stayed put."

Said Cyrus Eaton, another Nova Scotia-born financial giant: "I admired his genius." "Sure," said Alan Gordon, "Killam was a businessman, but he'd have fought to his last nickel to defend his principles." Said Nova Scotia's J.C. MacKeen: "He was perhaps one of the most remarkable personalities ever produced in this province if not in all Canada. His outstanding courage, analytical brain, imagination and energy were unsurpassed." Said Arthur Torrey: "If Ward Pitfield were alive he would say Killam was the most brilliant man he ever knew." Wrote Beaverbrook: "How I miss him."

As for Killam's views on Killam, perhaps someone summed it all up when he said: "Secretly, he was probably proud of what he'd done. But he never said."

For a generation that has come to take staggering federal deficits for granted, the most surprising thing about the Killam and Dunn estate taxes may be that, for a rather odd reason, they were a bit of an embarrassment to the government. It was already taking in more money than it was spending; it was running a surplus, and while this conformed to Keynesian theory as applied to good times it could also raise political problems. A surplus was an invitation to all sorts of people, including government supporters in the Commons, to come up with all sorts of ideas and pressures for spending the money. And now out of the blue had come these whopping additions.

It took some time for the government to decide what to do about it. Then on February 5, 1957, Prime Minister Louis St. Laurent rose in the Commons to make a surprising and unprecedented announcement. The federal treasury, he said, had been substantially enriched by duties imposed on two estates and the government proposed to use the money to help launch the Canada Council.

The idea had been in the offing ever since a Royal Commission under Rt. Hon. Vincent Massey had recommended in 1951 the establishment of such a body to nourish Canadian culture. Now the cabinet had decided to act.

St. Laurent named neither Killam nor Dunn but his references were obvious. His explanation was that the "windfall" from the two estates had had some influence on the decision to establish the Council with $50,000,000 as an endowment fund to provide scholarships in the humanities and social sciences and another $50,000,000 to provide universities, over a 10-year period, with capital assistance. The total of $100,000,000 would come out of a treasury running, he said, a surplus of between $300,000,000 and $400,000,000 and most of it would come from the two estates.

The windfall had come, said the Prime Minister, at a most opportune time. He wouldn't say that this was the governing consideration in the decision, but it was certainly a consideration. "I suppose," he added, "that there will be other windfalls because in spite of the rates of taxation there are growing fortunes in the hands of Canadian individuals." He hoped, too, that well-to-do people would make bequests to the Council.

The Prime Minister said one of the two men who had left this first windfall had said more than once that he was not making bequests to public institutions because succession duties were so high. If the government saw fit, he had been quoted as saying, it could use his duties to aid such institutions. The other had made modest contributions to similar institutions in his lifetime.

The decision to devote individual taxes to a specific end did set a precedent, and was viewed accordingly. One Tory Opposition member called it dangerous. One journalist called it "unexpected" and another called the prime minister's explanation "frank but nonetheless rather strange." Columnist George Bain found amusement in it. In an open letter to Finance Minister Walter Gordon, he said he'd been doing some free-lancing on the side and he'd like the extra tax he'd be paying to go (a) to buy an abacus for powerful cabinet minister C.D. Howe who "has never been very strong on figures in his off-the-cuff statements" and (b) to start a national collection of officialese, the stilted language of bureaucracy.

If the initial reaction to the announcement was surprise and, in some cases, scepticism, some of the long-range implications of the government action were different. It did get the Canada Council launched on a career that has poured millions into the intellectual stimulation of the country ever since. It also had an effect on the image of Izaak Walton Killam. If people were able to identify him in later years, it was apt to be as the man whose money had greatly helped to start the Council on its way, and this became more so as time forced the Council to live on government revenues. For large windfalls of estate taxes came no more, nor did the sort of gifts St. Laurent had hoped to see.

17

DOROTHY KILLAM AND

THE XYZs

It remained for Dorothy Johnston Killam to carry on the family name and reputation. In doing so, she became somewhat of an international celebrity, a figure of social consequence in Nassau, New York, on France's Riviera, became a favorite at times of those metropolitan gossip columnists who chronicled the functions and the foibles of the ultra-rich. She made news as the woman who not only tried to buy the Brooklyn Dodgers but later got involved in negotiations for a third major baseball league.

Only 55 when her husband died, she lived a full life despite her arthritis, her troubled back. She said she was "not going to be pushed around," hired her own lawyer and went her own way. She made her own fortune in time, from the schooling her husband had given her, from the sale of the empire he had left to her largely intact, from her own shrewdness, from good advice and straight-laced investments. Indeed, some of Killam's colleagues felt she had become the real power behind the throne even before he died. But Killam was her model. "He started by teaching me the ABCs of finance," she once said, "and by the time he died I had the XYZs." The record bears her out. She inherited more than $40,000,000 from her husband; when she died 10 years later her inheritance was heading towards $100,000,000.

She harvested one major advantage from the rising value of the stocks in her husband's companies. By April 1956 the stock of Calgary Power had risen from $39 a share to $59, of Mersey Paper from $170 to $225, of International Power from $188 to $240. Moreover, Mrs. Killam had put her shares in all three on the market, and she sold them all at a good, buoyant time to sell. From investments that had cost Killam much less, she gathered many millions.

When she put Mersey Paper on the block, the Toronto *Telegram* quoted financial circles as saying it was an event "unmatched in recent financial history. There isn't another instance in the world where a major paper mill could be purchased practically outright." There were 198,200 Mersey shares; she held 155,000 of them. The press said there were a number of bidders, but once Bowaters, the big British newsprint firm, revealed that it wanted to talk business, it became a question of reaching a mutually satisfactory price.

In one lawyer's opinion, Mrs. Killam did "a fantastic job" in making the sale: "She had facts at her fingertips. She had studied all the angles." The dickering took about a month and Bowaters' North American head, the prominent Montreal accountant George Currie, later chuckled that he always felt it was complicated by the fact a woman was involved: "We had a hard time getting her out of her swimming pools in Nassau to talk on the telephone." The negotiations ended, it is said, beside one of the two Nassau pools, with Mrs. Killam soothing her ailments in the water — as she regularly did — and Bowaters' men prowling the rims. She was, said Currie, "the dominating influence throughout." She got $230 a share, a total of some $35,000,000, for the firm Killam had launched into the teeth of the worst depression the world has known.

She sold International Power through Royal Securities to a group of American and Canadian investors. She peddled her stock in Price Brothers, it was said, by inviting the Toronto multi-millionaire industrialist E.P. Taylor over for lunch in Nassau, and telling him her husband would want him to have it. A later announcement said Taylor's St. Lawrence Corporation had bought her stock for $7,800,000.

In due course, from such sales, Mrs. Killam had tens of millions of dollars in liquid capital. She paid the estate duties and invested heavily, and the same sort of speculation, of tales, began to web around her name as they had around Killam's. It was said that she was playing the market; for one thing that she got in early on the stock of Metracal, a liquid food, and made a fortune. It wasn't true. She didn't play the market. Alan Gordon said she did meet a young businessman who reminded her of Killam, and discussed buying some of his company's stock so she could keep track of how he was doing. Her only problem was whether to buy 10 shares or 25. If she'd bought heavily, she would have made a fortune.

What she did invest in heavily was short-term bonds. They paid little interest, but that wasn't the point. The interest was taxable anyway. But a bond could be bought for less than it would be worth at maturity and at this stage there was no capital gains tax in Canada. She even bought an entire issue of Nova Scotia government bonds, and caused problems because she did it anonymously; Liberal Premier Henry Hicks was badgered by the Opposition to reveal who the mystery buyer was, and couldn't.

The capital of the estate Mrs. Killam would not touch. She felt, in the light of her husband's wishes, that she held it in trust; it would remain for the benefit of the country. But the income from the estate was more than enough to let her live grandly, and she did. She maintained the Montreal home and came there in summer. She spent the winters in Nassau, the springs in New York where she acquired the luxurious flat of the late Vincent Astor at 120 East End Ave. She also spent summers in Europe and on the Riviera.

She bought more jewelry. She entertained more than she had in her husband's lifetime.. "To go to one of her dinners," reminisced Paul Martin, long a Canadian cabinet minister, "was an unbelieveable experience. Unbelieveable! The setting. The servants. The guests. You met people there you could never hope to meet anywhere else. Interesting people. Famous people."

In the August 1960 issue of the *Ladies Home Journal* Mrs. Killam was grouped by writers Peter Briggs and Margaret Parton with others in an article on "The Richest Women in the World." It was heady company. Among them were Queen Elizabeth, former Queen Wilhelmina of the

Netherlands, Spain's beautiful duchess of Alba, England's Countess of Seafield whose "family history reaches back into the mists of time," a former Paris chorus girl and ballerina named Suzanna Voltera whose husband had left her $40,000,000, the Miss France of 1940 who became the wife and widow of Aga Khan III. The article said Mrs. Killam had been left perhaps $275,000,000 and that "some say she's a runner-up for the richest-woman-in-the-world sweepstakes." It described her as "a dainty, quick-humored woman who entertains moderately and dresses with quiet elegance." It told of her love of diamonds and baseball, and said she had once tried to buy the Brooklyn Dodgers for $8,000,000.

Although her lawyer said in later years that as far as he could see she was never really very serious about it, she once told a reporter that she had "kept on trying" to buy the Dodgers after Killam's death. She also said she had known all the top Dodgers officials, Branch Rickey, Walter O'Malley, among others, all their managers from Leo (Lippy) Durocher to Walt Alston, and most of their top players. Their star shortstop, that former Montreal Royal Jackie Robinson, once presented her with the bat with which he made the hit that won one world series.

It was O'Malley, called the "most influential and controversial figure in baseball," who told writer Gerald Holland how he first became aware of Mrs. Killam's interest in buying the Dodgers. Holland's article in the July 13, 1968 issue of *The Saturday Evening Post* said:

> Shortly after O'Malley had become president she fell head over heals in love with the Dodgers. She attended every home game and one time, during spring training, she invited O'Malley, his wife Kay and anyone else they cared to bring to visit her for cocktails and dinner at her winter home in Nassau. O'Malley accepted and loaded the Dodgers' big plane with as many of his friends as he could round up in a hurry.
>
> "It was the greatest party I ever saw," O'Malley recalled. "There were more servants around than ice cubes. Mrs. Killam told of her great devotion to our ball club and then, in the manner of a charming hostess putting her guests at their ease with small talk, she said

151

'Mr. O'Malley, would you consider an offer of five million dollars for an interest in the team?'

"I was stunned to say the least," he said. "I dropped my drink in the lady's lap. As servants came running from all directions, Mrs. Killam just acted as if nothing had happened. When I got over my embarrassment I told her I was very sorry that there was no Dodgers' stock presently available. I added that if the situation changed I would let her know immediately."

O'Malley told Holland Mrs. Killam's arrival at any New York ball park spread through the grapevine of ushers and attendants before her chauffeur had time to shut off the motor of her car. "She threw money around so freely," he said, "that in time a $10 tip came to be regarded as a sort of rebuke for poor service."

One of her servants once described these baseball outings as picnics. She took along guests, at least one servant, supplies of food and drink. She had her own box seats. She kept her own score card, watched the play with an expert's knowledge. Once, said O'Malley, she asked New York Giants owner Horace Stoneham what he'd want for that "attractive young man" who was pitching for them that day. Stoneham said he wasn't for sale but, if he was, the price might be up to $100,000. Mrs. Killam said she'd write a cheque immediately. "Madam," said Stoneham, "if you're looking for an escort or dancing partner I suggest you look elsewhere."

As O'Malley told the story, "Mrs. Killam looked at Stoneham with absolute loathing, then said, 'Mr. Stoneham, I am in no need of escorts or dancing partners. I was interested in buying your pitcher to present as a gift to my friend Mr. Walter O'Malley. He needs pitching in Brooklyn. Good day, sir!' "

Not long after it became obvious in 1956 that the Dodgers would be moving to Los Angeles, someone is said to have asked Mrs. Killam whether she would now bid for Stoneham's Giants to prevent them, in turn, from decamping to San Francisco. "The Giants," she snapped, "I wouldn't pay a nickel for them." As for the New York Yankees, then the perennial champions of the American League, she disliked them too; they beat the Dodgers too often in the world series.

When the Cleveland Indians got into a tight pennant race with the Yankees in 1954 she began to root for them. Hank Greenberg, the former home-run king who had become general manager of the Indians, said her first call made him suspect someone was pulling his leg. A woman's voice he'd never heard before said she was at her fishing camp, that radio reception wasn't too good and she was having trouble keeping abreast of the pennant race. "She said," reported Greenberg, "that she hoped I wouldn't mind if she phoned every day." She did, and when the Indians won the pennant she asked if he could arrange to get her a number of box seats for the world series. By now Greenberg was hooked. "Such faith," he said, "should be rewarded. I was only too happy to oblige. That's when I met her. She's a really exciting lady." When Mrs. Killam did arrive she had both servants and guests with her.

She never missed a world series if she could possibly get there, and against such a background it was hardly surprising when in 1959 she became involved in plans for placing a team in a new major league to be called the Continental. When the news broke, a *Gazette* sportswriter said it was hoped she represented Montreal, and she did tell a reporter that year that both Montreal and Toronto were "wonderful sports towns" which would, without doubt, support major league baseball. But her eyes were on New York.

On June 18 Bill Shea, the chairman of New York Mayor Robert Wagner's Baseball Committee, revealed the names of members of a syndicate said to have pledged $4,500,000 to back a New York entry in the new league. One was Dorothy Killam. One was Mrs. Charles Shipman Payson, the former Joan Whitney, who *had* tried to buy the Giants in 1957 to prevent their departure, and who still held a substantial block of Giants stock. The third millionaire principal was Dwight F. Davis, jr., son of the donor of the Davis Cup, premier prize of international tennis. There were three others behind them but the two women alone, said *Sports Illustrated*, each had "a dowry fat enough to choke an umpire," and each was escorted by a small army from the "top drawer of the sporting aristocracy." Ladies Day, said the magazine, "is really here."

The January 16, 1960, issue of *Maclean's* magazine said "when and if baseball's third major league gets off the drawing board, one third of the money and a great deal of the enthusiasm behind its most important entry will come from what is at first glance a highly unlikely source: the distinguished, seldom-heard-of dowager of the biggest fortune ever left in Canada." Dorothy Killam, it said "may easily be the most dedicated woman baseball buff in history."

Nevertheless, Mrs. Killam's enthusiasm for the New York franchise didn't last. She changed her mind and withdrew from the negotiations, for tax reasons, for health reasons — as she neared 60 she was starting to search for peace and quiet — and to some extent because she didn't like the idea of having partners; if she was going to be associated with a baseball team, she wanted to own all of it or nothing.

As things turned out, the Continental League never got off the ground. But the New York team did. It became today's Mets of the National League.

At one stage in the baseball negotiations of 1959, Mrs. Killam was reported to be on the Riviera, as she was in other years. That year the London *Evening Standard* reported the social season "glitters brilliantly; small fortunes are changing hands in the casinos," and Dorothy Killam was staying at Cap Ferrat with Lady Kenmare. She liked the Riviera, and she began looking for a suitable home there after some years of renting. In 1963 she did something that surprised even the sophisticated.

The New York *Journal-American's* society columnist "Suzy Knickerbocker" wrote that "those glittering international socialites, Gianni and Mariella Agnelli (Fiat money and everything that goes with it)" were trying to peddle their Villa Leopolda, "the most breathtaking, lavish, most publicized villa in the South of France," and that Mrs. Killam was reported to be interested. But, it was added, she appeared to have decided the price, $3,000,000, was "too much even for the likes of her. And the likes of her is quite something."

Eventually Suzy Knickerbocker said Mrs. Killam had finally decided to buy La Leopolda; the price was unknown but "I'll bet it wasn't $3,000,000. It may be the rich, rich, rich world of Dorothy Killam, but it's not that mad." It was though. Another New York columnist, "Cholly Knickerbocker," reported that she *had* paid $3,000,000, for what had been

154

"summer headquarters for the really 'in' members of the International Smart Set," and he was right. Mrs. Killam seemed compelled, he wrote, to be "one of the world's foremost hostesses . . . Sixtyish and very well liked, Dorothy's Renaissance good looks and Renaissance largesse help make her a natural for the place she may wish to take in society" though she was still "a rather unknown figure."

Soon thereafter yet another society columnist, Jerome Zerbe, reported her "happily ensconsed" and that La Leopolda had been returned to the estate it must have been when it was owned by King Leopold of Belgium — reputedly as a sanctuary for his mistress. "There she is with her entourage, and Monsieur Boudin of Jansen, Paris, has redone several rooms." Yet Mrs. Killam wasn't entertaining the sort of crowds the Agnellis had catered to. Indeed, the villa was "a little overpowering today when only a dozen people sit down for a meal in a huge dinning room that would be happier with 30 or more."

La Leopolda *was* an overpowering place, an incredible 25-acre place where the butler had a home of his own, called La Solitude. From a setting in the hills, it had a spectacular view of the Mediterranean and Cap Ferrat. The long flight of steps that led up to it was made famous by the movie "Red Shoes" which was filmed there. When the daughter of a doctor at the Montreal Neurological Institute visited Mrs. Killam she was so charmed by her hostess, so awed by the environment that she came home, said her father, "feeling like Cinderella. It took her days to settle down."

The villa, wrote Zerbe in later years, had "a serene, classical facade" and "on warm days one lunches on the broad terrace or sips a drink while watching the sun set." Mrs. Killam not only had Stefane Boudin in to redecorate some of the rooms, she added a new wing to "provide dining space for her 12 upstairs servants." In the main dining room there were superb white-and-gold Empire chairs and "here, as in other rooms, massed flowers, fresh every day from the gardens, provide the color one associates with the Riviera."

Here, in a home once owned by an eccentric king who wanted his morning newspaper pressed before it was brought up with breakfast, Dorothy Killam found the crowning expression of her romantic tastes. She brought along her cherished Vigée-Lebrun portrait of Marie Antoinette. It dominated one of many walls.

Her homes, her social life, her personality, her devotion to baseball once led a reporter to describe her as "one of the great Canadian eccentrics, a woman of decisive taste and extravagant gesture." Some people considered her vain, egocentric, snobbish, "a woman with a terrible conceit," a woman with great social ambitions "who wanted only money and got what she wanted," a woman who liked to make other women satellites. But people who knew her well, who generally liked and admired her, told a different story. She did, as one friend put it, "have expensive, expansive and wealthy tastes," but there was more to her than that. She was a lady. She liked good manners, good dress, good taste. She disliked vulgarity and rough talk. She was fussy in picking guests and she was apt to invite them to come at 8 o'clock for dinner, have one cocktail and get to the table within 15 minutes; she didn't like too much drinking. She liked conservative people, had little use for many who were considered socialites.

To a senior Royal Securities executive, she was an even more remarkable person than her husband. To Paul Martin, "once you got to know her you found she was a really pleasant woman, a fine, simple woman, interested in the world around her." To a distinguished lawyer she was "essentially a humble and sincere Christian person" who could spend hours chatting in the home of her gardener in Nassau, who did numerous quiet kindnesses such as arranging for a Bahamas girl from a modest home to go to college in Canada.

She took for years a great interest in the opera, was a member of the board of the New York Metropolitan Opera, contributed handsomely each year to its funds. She financed new productions of Bellini's "La Sonnambula" and Richard Strauss' "Die Frau Ohne Schatten," helped finance a Montreal appearance of the great Australian coloratura, Joan Sutherland. She loved to go to the Met. "She loved opera for opera's sake," a friend on its board said. "She loved its music and its drama. She was interested in the many problems we had at the Metropolitan. My wife and I have sat for hours talking with her about one artist after another, their careers, their voices and artistry, their personal problems."

156

For years she was limited in what she could do as her arthritis grew severe. For a long time, a doctor said, she suffered a lot more pain than people knew because she bore it well and kept it to herself. She felt the cold bitterly and often sat wrapped in furs at the Met or at the bridge tables in Nassau. She needed the help of a cane and often of a wheelchair.

She continued to swim a lot because it helped fight her illness. Though it was a long time since she had trained American frogmen for World War II service, it was swimming that extended her life in her declining years, just as fishing had extended her husband's. And the old competitive streak still burned in her. When she went to the lodge on the Cascapedia in the late '50s she insisted on going fishing though her condition was such that the guides had to build a special rail to help her down to the water and a special canoe seat so she could handle a line.

She went out that way, and it turned out to be a momentous occasion. There were two guides with her but, as they helped her, they didn't see something she did: the leap of a salmon downstream. She told them to take her to the spot, and there she hooked a salmon and brought it in. It weighed 46 pounds, more than any her husband had ever killed. She was so happy she promptly gave the guides a $1,000 tip and her joy was enlarged when Alan Gordon, one of her guests, sent the details to an American sporting magazine. Hers won a $100 prize as the biggest salmon killed that year. But she never tried fishing again. Her arthritis made it too painful, too difficult.

She came to suspect that the disease would ultimately confine her permanently to bed or wheelchair, and for that reason and others she erected walls around her privacy. She found she had to. They were primarily a reaction to siege. Because she had so much money she became the focus of persistent attention, sometimes by people looking for handouts, frequently by spokesmen seeking help for worthy causes. All sorts of hopes that had been crushed by her husband's will sprang back to vigorous life at the prospects of a second chance. Simply to prevent the onslaughts from overrunning her life, she did erect barriers around her, used her lawyer, Donald Byers of Montreal, to sort out approaches.

Some got through the barriers, and failed; one scholarly president of a Maritime university spent hours boning up on baseball before talking to Mrs. Killam; it did him little or no good. Some got through and thought erroneously that they had succeeded; another university president felt he came away with a vague promise of millions; one of his fundraisers would later dwell on "the nightmare" of how it all fell through.

Some didn't have to go through the barriers at all. The wealthy Mrs. Jules Timmins of Montreal called Mrs. Killam "a wonderful friend" and said she could always be counted on for an annual gift for retarded children. Some didn't have to go through, and still failed. One, according to Toronto communications magnate John W. Bassett, was Lord Beaverbrook. Bassett was among a number of guests of Beaverbrook in Nassau, and their host told them he wanted to get Killam money for the University of New Brunswick. He primed his guests, all men of distinction, told them what he wanted them to do, and then invited Mrs. Killam in for dinner. The dinner was splendid, and she was the only woman there, and she liked that. The men were all dressed up, and they were as charming as they could be, and she enjoyed every minute of it. It developed subtly into a battle of wits, and she won. "She handled every one of us," Bassett grinned. "It was beautiful. Beautiful!" She left without promising a dime, and when she'd gone Beaverbrook shook his head and said, "She beat us all." Said Bassett in admiration: "She could handle herself in any company."

She surprised various businessmen with her knowledge of business and finance. One was Sydney Frost, president of the Bank of Nova Scotia, who visited her in Nassau as an emissary for Acadia University and with one special credential to help: he'd gone to school in Yarmouth with Killam though he'd been in a lower grade. He got something for Acadia, he later said, but not nearly what he had hoped. But what amazed him was seeing Mrs. Killam at dinner one evening, moving from one table to another, talking business with male guests: "She really knew what she was talking about."

Beyond everything else she applied that knowledge to thinking out, planning what to do about the mandate her husband had given her: to pass on their money to worthy causes when she was through with it. She knew, above all, that he wanted it to remain in Canada, with an emphasis on Nova

158

Scotia. He had never indicated that he regretted not having gone to college, but he had singled out higher education as the main instrument to fulfill his designs. He wanted to advance it particularly in the fields of medicine, science and engineering. He was against putting money he had made into buildings, into capital expenditures.

With the advice of Byers, her chief executor, and others, Mrs. Killam took it from there. Step by step, year by year, she gradually developed her will. There were numerous changes, in effect a whole series of wills. Something she put in one year, she might take out the next. "She was very interested in the whole thing," Byers said. "She felt she had the money in trust, and she wanted the capital to go where she felt her husband would approve." Beneath it all, the general plan was always fixed: the emphasis would be on scholarships at the post-graduate level. Beneath that again was another idea: like her husband, keen American though she was, she hoped to do something to help stop Canada's brain drain to the United States. She wanted to encourage promising young Canadians to stay at home and she felt she could help by providing more adequate facilities for advanced study.

For a time she thought of establishing a foundation, then decided it didn't make sense when the institutions she wanted to help would remain in being. She'd give them money, tell them what she wanted to do, leave the rest to them. Because she wanted to experiment with her ideas, to see how they would work, she made — anonymously — two handsome gifts in 1962-63; she took $8,500,000 worth of redeemable preferred shares in an investment company and split them in two.

One half went as a contribution to the Canada Council, the interest on which was to finance advanced study or research in medicine, science and engineering by Canadians in Canada. She wanted, she said, "to help build Canada's future." It was the largest gift the Council had ever received from one donor, and it brought from the *Montreal Star* an editorial tribute which said "it opens the door to a broad new field for the agency which has hitherto been concerned essentially with the humanities." The *Star* hoped, without much success, that it would "encourage others to think along similar lines."

159

The second gift went to Dalhousie, the Halifax university to which she had already given nearly $400,000 in the past five years and which awarded her an honorary degree of doctor of civil laws in 1962. Said the citation: "Although she received a fine humanistic education and might lay some claim to being a Latin scholar, her ruling passion has been in expanding the wealth of nations in her husband's name, content that the credit should all be his for achievements in which she was at least an equal architect." She was, it added, "a wise consort of a great merchant prince, and a builder of Canadian wealth in her own right."

The Dalhousie gift was a sign that increasingly her thoughts were turning to her husband's native province, that it was there that she would concentrate a large part of her estate. Up to 1963, she did spend part of each year in Montreal. She maintained her ties with the Montreal Neurological Institute, continued to be a patient there from time to time. One of its doctors continued to be her doctor. She relied on its nurses, wired from Europe on occasion to have one sent over. When her friend Eileen Flanagan retired as director of nursing in 1961 and the staff gave a dinner in her honor, Mrs. Killam showed up unexpectedly. "She looked radiant," said Miss Flanagan, "in a dark dress, with her jewels." She sat next to Dr. Penfield and she was asked to say a few words. She declined. Her husband, she smiled, had told her never to speak in public.

In 1963, the year she bought La Leopolda, she also decided that the time had come to shift her official domicile out of Montreal. She considered moving it to Nassau or Switzerland but came to the conclusion that it should remain in Canada. By the end of 1963 she had signed an agreement to sell the Sherbrooke Street home Killam had bought 43 years before. The sale itself went through in March 1964. That December she signed a lease for a large penthouse apartment in Halifax. She had changed her domicile.

She left Montreal with Quebec in the midst of its Quiet Revolution and, she left, one lawyer said, mainly for taxation reasons. But when it became known that, apart from one gift to a very special institution, her will did nothing for the city where she'd lived for decades there were those who suspected she'd never forgotten that slight from the Mount Royal Club.

18

THE PRINCELY GIFTS

When Mrs. Killam descended — the word fetches not too far — upon Halifax in the spring of 1965, Donald McInnes, Q.C., was at the airport to greet her in a double capacity. He was her Halifax lawyer and he was chairman of the board of governors of Dalhousie University at a time when it had high hopes that she would be kind to it.

She would, as it turned out, but what McInnes remembered most vividly was her arrival itself. She had asked him to get a vehicle to take luggage into town, and he no sooner reached the airport than he realized that he had underestimated in hiring a van. Mrs. Killam's very correct butler was already on hand. He knew his lady. He knew her entourage and what luggage they'd have. He took one look at the van and pronounced it inadequate. They hastily set about finding and hiring a truck, and by the time Mrs. Killam's plane landed Donald McInnes was in a state approaching trauma.

Then she swept off and into his ample limousine and restored him to beaming tranquillity with one smiling sentence: "My, Mr. McInnes, how young you look." She could, despite her ailments, still do these things. In the opinion of high society's Mrs. J.C. MacKeen she even did it to the city itself: "She devastated Halifax."

She was there less than two weeks but in that time she joined the First Baptist Church and two clubs, examined the penthouse acquired for her and pronounced it, as her butler had the van, inadequate, talked of renting a floor of the Nova Scotian Hotel, was wined and dined, and above all else looked into the affairs of two institutions that had captured her interest.

One was the local Children's Hospital, and the story of Mrs. Killam's connection with it had started some time earlier. The hospital was housed in a dowdy old building which its board had hoped to reconstruct, only to be advised by a consultant that it would be far better to tear it down and start all over again. The board had started the campaign for a modest $6,000,000, not because that's what they needed but because that was all they felt able to collect. A drive for funds was organized under Maj-Gen. E.C. Plow, only recently retired as Nova Scotia's Lieutenant Governor. In the course of his duties, he asked J.C. MacKeen where he might get financial help, and MacKeen had a magic piece of advice. He said he'd just been talking to Dorothy Killam in New York, and that she wanted to build a memorial to her husband in his native province.

An appointment was made, and a delegation flew to New York to meet her. They found her sufficiently interested to promise that she'd give them an immediate $75,000, and that she'd look into the matter further. She carried things a step forward by inviting General Plow, Halifax architect Andris Kundzins and Toronto hospital consultant Arthur H. Peckham to visit her in Nassau. There they found that she had her own ideas and that she would be coming to Halifax.

When she arrived they had a model of the proposed hospital to show her. It was not designed as the memorial she wanted, and she said she'd have none of it. She had far more expansive ideas. At the moment, they staggered the board. They had planned to have the building face in one direction; she wanted it to face in another, to provide a sweeping entrance, to have it look out on what would become the axis of an enlarged complex of buildings associated with Dalhousie University. There was next door the rundown old Halifax Mental Hospital; it had been condemned and she wanted it removed. She did not think it was a good thing to have next to a children's hospital. She wanted a memorial lobby to honor her husband. She wanted other changes, and she said she was willing to put up $5,000,000. The board said the changes would be made.

She became enthusiastic about the whole thing. While it was true that the project ran counter to her husband's dislike of putting money into buildings, she decided this was to be an exception. She wanted a physical monument to him, with a memorial lobby to make it explicit.

The second institution was Dalhousie itself, and she went about her study of it in the same thorough way. She said she was there to carry out her husband's wishes to help it. She spent hours with its president, Dr. Henry Hicks, and with Donald McInnes, went all over the campus, asked questions and formed opinions "in a highly intelligent manner," gained an insight into its plans, its buildings and their functions. She liked what she saw. She reconfirmed her intention to give Dalhousie a large portion of her estate, and she came to call it "my great love."

On May 26 she left to fly to New York. It was her intention to summer at La Leopolda, to return to Halifax in the fall and then go to Nassau for the winter. She got to La Leopolda in June and she lived fairly actively. Her secretary could only wonder at her energy as guests came and went: "It was painful for her just to get up. A lot of people would have given up, but not her."

Mrs. Killam entertained. Even now she couldn't resist the impulse to be dramatic. One evening her guests were having drinks when, very quietly, two large doors opened at the end of a palatial room — one knew they were propelled by human hands but one couldn't see them — and she made her belated and bejewelled entrance. Every eye in the room followed her across the space between them. She enjoyed the majestic view. She swam. She had Kundzins and Peckham fly over and she showed them some of the architectural features of her villa which she wanted built into the new Children's Hospital. She wanted other changes. "She even made changes in her changes," said Kundzins.

Sometimes in these discussions she was difficult. Sometimes she was understanding. Sometimes she fired people, then took them back. The fact was that she was failing fast, and in the last half of July she became so ill that she had to stay in bed. Doctors were called in and hovered over her. Nurses maintained a round-the-clock watch. Donald Byers was summoned from Montreal and found her very weak from internal bleeding but still anxious to talk.

She wired, then called Henry Hicks in Halifax and said she wanted to build on the Dalhousie campus a second memorial to her husband. She said she was thinking of a headquarters for post-graduate education, the field in which most of her money would be spent. Hicks knew the university needed a library more, and he proposed that as an alternative. The post-graduate headquarters, he said, could be housed there if she wished. She wanted to know where the building would go and when he told her she said she could picture it exactly. She asked about the cost, and he said it would be at least $5,000,000. She said that was fine.

She called Donald McInnes too, and told him she was going to change her will once more, and leave everything to Dalhousie. It never came to pass. She did call Byers in about five o'clock one morning and say she wished to make one change: she wanted to leave $1,000,000 to the two children of a friend. It was the final fairytale act in a fairytale life. She wasn't up to making the changes she had envisaged for Dalhousie.

Late in the afternoon of July 26 she said she'd like to leave her bed and have tea on the terrace overlooking the sea. A doctor said it was a strange thing but just before they died some people felt they wanted to do something active like this. Instead, she went back to sleep. Later the internal bleeding recommenced and about 1:30 on the morning of July 27 she died.

She had said more than once that she had lied so often about her age that she was no longer sure just how old she was. At death she was, in fact, 65.

Wrote society columnist Suzy Knickerbocker: "She will be missed."

Dorothy Killam died proud of the fact that in 10 years she had seen her estate surpass the one her husband had left. It amounted to some $93,000,000 at the time of her death, and it was still growing. Only a small portion was taxable;

governments took roughly $6,000,000 of it for estate duties on personal bequests. The rest went, tax-free, to institutions.

Donald McInnes, in announcing the details of her will shortly after she was buried in Halifax, called its gifts "princely," and they were. But it went beyond that. Firmly based on Killam's intentions, it reflected the years of thought that had gone into it. It was detailed in its complexity, precise in its instructions, even historic in its implications. It also was flexible enough to be workable.

Mrs. Killam had had money enough to think very large thoughts, and she did. She wanted, in her own words, "to help in the building of Canada's future by encouraging advanced study." She wanted to do things that would compare with or even surpass the famed program of scholarships bequeathed to England's Oxford University by South Africa's Cecil Rhodes. In her bequest to Dalhousie University alone, she topped Rhodes' total gift of years before. She gave it, including the anonymous gift of 1962, some $30,000,000, probably the largest donation to a university in Canadian history. She gave some $14,000,000 to the University of British Columbia, in the province where Killam had made money out of pulp and paper. She gave some $16,000,000 to the University of Alberta and the University of Calgary in the province where Calgary Power flourished. She gave the new Izaak Walton Killam Hospital for Children in Halifax another $3,000,000 to add to the $5,000,000 already promised. She gave some $15,000,000 to the Canada Council, including the anonymous gift in 1962. She gave the Montreal Neurological Institute some $4,000,000, and members of its staff considered it a tribute to a number of people there who won the Killams' affection and admiration. Today in its entrance there is a plaque which reads: "The Izaak Walton Killam Memorial Endowment Fund and Fund for Advanced Studies were established in 1966 at the Montreal Neurological Institute by the bequest of Dorothy Johnston Killam 'to help in the building of Canada's future by encouraging advanced study.' In years to come those who turn to research and teaching in the M.N.I. will make their contribution to the wellbeing of mankind with the continuing help of Izaak and Dorothy Killam." The bequest — the only one to any institution in Monteal — was considerably larger than the donation Dr. Penfield had sought years before and at the bottom of that plaque there is an intriguing quotation from Rudyard Kipling's *The Explorer* which Penfield himself selected. Its reference is to medical research but for the gentle "beggar" perhaps it had a wider significance. "Something hidden," it says. "Go and find it."

Mrs. Killam's will laid stress on people. It laid stress on medical, scientific and engineering education and research, mainly because she felt the money put into the Canada Council from her husband's succession duties had made its contribution to the arts. It was so designed that its benefits would go on for years through interest payments on the capital she wanted kept intact.

The bequests fell under a number of headings. For Dalhousie, as the outstanding case, one section was designed to provide income for two Killam Memorial Chairs in advanced study in science and/or engineering, to attract "men of the highest distinction" to hold them. One section provided a Killam Memorial Salary Fund to help pay the salaries of permanent teaching staff exclusive of the arts. A third provided the Izaak Walton Killam Memorial Fund, otherwise known as a Killam Trust, and the purpose again was "to help in the building of Canada's future by encouraging advanced study" through scholarships. Like other parts of the will, this third type of bequest was also made to other institutions and, in making them, Mrs. Killam said, "I hope in some measure to increase the scientific and scholastic attainments of Canadians, to develop and expand the work of Canadian Universities, and to promote sympathetic understanding between Canadians and people of other countries. Accordingly, the net income from each Killam Trust shall be used to provide fellowships and other grants (all to be known as 'Killam Scholarships' . . .) for advanced study or research at universities or hospitals, research or scientific institutes, or other equivalent or similar institutions both in Canada and in other countries in any field of study or research other than the arts as presently defined in the Canada Council Act and not limited to the 'humanities and social sciences' referred to in such Act."

The scholarships, insofar as possible, should "be granted for work either leading or subsequent to a doctorate or for work of similar standing." But a Killam Scholar "should not be a one-sided person and each scholar's special distinction of intellect should be founded upon sound character and good manners. No person shall be qualified or disqualified as a Killam scholar on account of his or her race or religious opinions." The scholarships, further, may be granted "to suitable candidates from outside Canada as well as Canadians," but the non-Canadians should study or do research in Canada.

The impact of the will has been enormous. In the words of Dr. Henry Hicks, it enabled Dalhousie to "play in the big leagues of post-graduate education" for the first time. Said Dr. Walter H. Gage, president of the University of British Columbia in the '70s: "These funds enabled the University . . . to attract outstanding scholars . . . to offer assistance to promising graduate students and to give much needed assistance to those engaged in valuable research in a variety of fields. Funds such as these are enabling the University of British Columbia to play an increasingly important role in the development of Canada." To Dr. M. Wyman, then president of the University of Alberta, the money "has been extremely useful in providing two Killam Chairs for the University, providing a variety of scholarships, and generally useful in improving this University in many ways."

In these institutions and others the money has helped keep at home young Canadians who might have left to study elsewhere. It has also attracted to Canada both outstanding teachers and young people who come to learn. The University of Calgary, as one example, soon made Killam awards not only to Canadians but to Americans, Britons, Africans, Asiatics and Australians. In the '80s a University of Alberta spokesman said it could not call itself an "international university" if its Killam funds did not exist.

Nowhere was the will's impact greater than at The Izaak Walton Killam Hospital for Children in Halifax. The $8,000,000 gift was only part of the $21,000,000 it ultimately cost, but it played a major role in transforming it into one of the outstanding institutions in its field. It made possible a far larger hospital than originally planned, immense development of laboratories vital to diagnosis of diseases and for research, and "every modern device for surgery and treatment of children." The effect, said Dr. R.B. Goldbloom who left the Montreal Children's Hospital to become its first physician-in-chief, was "a total revolution." It made the hospital one of *the* places to study children's diseases, launched research in a variety of fields, attracted budding doctors from various parts of Canada and elsewhere, and placed at the disposal of all the Atlantic Provinces the facilities of a major institution.

For the Canada Council, the bequests permitted the establishment of three categories of awards, senior research scholarships in the humanities and social sciences, post-doctoral research scholarships for "freely initiated cross-disciplinary work combining a scholar's area of specialization with any other area of study," and I.W. Killam Memorial scholarships to encourage research and advanced studies in science, engineering and medicine. These allowed some of the winners to free themselves of their academic and administrative duties for considerable periods of time. Within relatively few years the Council's awards had run well into the millions of dollars, and as high as $378,000 for a single project. By 1985 it began, among other things, to offer three annual Killam Memorial prizes of $50,000 each to eminent scholars in the fields of engineering and the natural and health sciences.

At the Montreal Neurological Institute in the '70s Dr. William Feindel, its director, said the Killam money "came at a critical time, when research costs were going up and it was difficult to keep young Canadians at home. They were going south in droves." The funds helped both to staunch that flow and to attract people to Canada. In the '80s, Dr. Feindel spoke of "the remarkable impact" of the Killam will on post-graduate studies in Canada, said the M.N.I. had been able to attract bright young physician-scientists at the post-doctoral stage, had provided them with personnel and research support "to establish a base of operations" and found that many "then succeeded in gaining highly competitive awards outside the institute." Their work at the M.N.I. over the years "provides an exciting example of the variety of disciplines now being applied to investigation of the nervous system."

By the mid-'80s the number of Killam Scholars at the various institutions had grown to some 4,000 and the awards they had received were approaching $50,000,000. They had become prestigious figures on the intellectual landscape. Like Izaak Walton Killam's own career, the program his wife designed was shaped for, was continuing for the long haul. Without uttering a single word publicly, the reticent "tightwad" had had his final say.

19

EPILOGUE

The story of Izaak Walton and Dorothy Johnston Killam is a case study of a phenomenon of a society that is nominally capitalist but becoming less so. So is the reaction to them. What time will do to their names only time itself can tell. In a society which increasingly accepts governmental intervention in its economy and its life, which has produced big government and the welfare state, which lives off business yet is sceptical of those who grow rich from it, is sceptical of business itself and of many other things once taken for granted, which has spawned the faceless corporation and anonymous investment funds to supersede individual giants, which has built computers to do the sort of things Killam did in his head, in such a society the years have already put a new perspective on many of the things he and his wife thought and did. A century after Killam's birth, inflation and change were reflected in a federal deficit close to 1,000 times larger than that total federal budget which had agitated the Yarmouth *Herald* in 1885. Thirty years after his death the wealth that had made him known as "the richest man in Canada" would no longer come near to justifying the claim.

Yet the Killams remain one of the most remarkable couples Canada has ever known — exceptionally gifted in some ways, limited in others, individualists to the core, both of them. They built a substantial empire which tapped and produced great wealth, provided jobs for thousands and survived through cruel turns of economic fortune; its component parts thrive still. In life they were by some accounted selfish because they kept so much of the proceeds for themselves. In life and mainly in death, through the use of taxes and bequests, they lavished some $125,000,000 upon the land that had chiefly made it possible, and virtually all of it went into that realm of advanced scholarship neither of them had ever known.

Their name now is commemorated in three physical structures, The Izaak Walton Killam Hospital for Children in Halifax and two others. One is Dalhousie's great stone Killam Library. The university did use some Killam income for one of its funds to help build it but most of the capital came from government grants. Today a plaque says it is dedicated to the two Killams in gratitude for their gifts to the university. The other structure is a handsome library in Yarmouth, built through the gift of Killam's two sisters. It overlooks the main street where he and his newsboys peddled papers many years ago.

The images of Killam and his wife still mean different things to different people. When the Halifax *Chronicle-Herald* in 1971 ran a laudatory full-page article on Killam, a Grade 12 girl in Yarmouth retorted sharply by letter that he may have had, as it stated, a "deep love for Canada" and "a special affection for Nova Scotia . . . but Yarmouth seems not to have merited his attention." For years obscurity clung to their names in many cases. Many people who received their scholarships had no idea who they were; some misspelled their name. At Bowater-Mersey Paper's headquarters near Liverpool there was no picture of the man who started it. In Alberta, in British Columbia where former Killam industries flourished, his name meant little or nothing.

On faded, jaded St. James Street the headquarters where he laid his plans stood gnarled and empty, its musty panelling and antique bond cages gathering grime. On Sherbrooke Street the house where he lived for 35 years stood empty too until it was destroyed to make way for the remorseless march of skyscrapers. In a single sale, the famous collection of jewelry passed into the hands of New York's

171

Harry Winston, Inc. La Leopolda, the Nassau properties, the fishing camps came to be owned by others. Their furniture had been sold or given to servants. The beloved Vigée-Lebrun painting of Marie Antoinette adorned a wall at Dalhousie.

The Killam empire itself passed into various hands, a good part of it into the American control he himself had resisted. International Power and the B.C. Pulp and Paper properties both did. Mersey went its way in British and American hands. Royal Securities was bought by New York's Merrill Lynch, Pierce, Fenner and Smith in 1969. At the time, 14 years after Killam's death, Alexander Ross of the *Financial Post* wrote, "it's difficult to think of Royal Securities without thinking of the canny Maritimer who made the firm what it was . . . Trite as it may sound, the end of Royal Securities as an autonomous investment house really is the end of an era, or something. Or maybe the era ended when Izaak Killam died, and nobody's acknowledged it till now." The very term Royal Securities was kept in the firm's title well into the '80s, then dropped because there was no easy or satisfactory way to express the French equivalent required by Quebec law.

Looking back over it all in his late 70s, one retired Royal Securities executive found it regrettable that some people thought ill of the Killam who had put all this together in the first place. "All I can say," he mused, "is that I think that anyone who ever worked for him admired him." In Halifax, Mrs. MacKeen said that never had she seen such a change in a public image as the one she had seen emerge after the announcement of Mrs. Killam's will.

For one group of people, there were no doubts. They were the servants who worked for the couple for years in Montreal and elsewhere. Two or three of them had made a pilgrimage to Halifax each year to visit the cemetery where Mrs. Killam was buried and where she had had her husband's body moved from Montreal to lie beside her. When one former servant made one such trip, he visited the marbled lobby of the Children's Hospital with its posthumous painting of Killam by Britain's Simon Elwes, and nearly broke down. "I could see her in the whole concept of this hospital," he said.

When she went to the cemetery, as she had done a number of times, a little maid named May Grieve had much the same reaction. She remembered Killam as "every inch a gentleman." She remembered Mrs. Killam as "a very fine person," like no one else she had ever met. She remembered both of them with affection because "they made us a happy home." And as she stood beside their graves, she confided with the soft burr of Scotland in her voice, "I always said a little prayer — and I always felt she knew we were there."

The Author

Douglas How grew up in Dorchester, N.B., and in 1937, at 18, became a reporter with the Moncton *Daily Times*. He was a soldier and then a war correspondent in World War II. From 1945-53 he was with The Canadian Press in the parliamentary press gallery in Ottawa and later was executive assistant to Hon. Robert Winters, Nova Scotia's representative in the cabinet. He worked for *Time* magazine in Ottawa, Toronto and New York and was in charge of its Canadian correspondents prior to serving for 10 years as Canadian editor of *Reader's Digest* in Montreal. He was the editor-in-chief of the *Digest's* three-volume set of books on Canada in the war, is the author of a regimental history and of an earlier, privately-circulated biography of the Killams. At 52, he graduated from Mount Allison University, later was on its staff for three years, then went back to what he most enjoys: writing. He now resides with his wife in St. Andrews, N.B.